Towards a
Freer Curriculum

H. G. Macintosh and
L. A. Smith

UNIVERSITY OF LONDON PRESS LTD

ISBN 0 340 16773 4 Boards
ISBN 0 340 16774 2 Unibook

University of London Press Ltd
St Paul's House, Warwick Lane, London EC4P 4AH

Printed in Great Britain by
Butler & Tanner Ltd, Frome and London

Contents

Acknowledgments

The authors would like to record their particular thanks to the following: L. A. Smith's colleagues at the Curriculum Laboratory, University of London Goldsmiths' College, Charity James and Edwin Mason; the late B. C. Lucia, Secretary to the Associated Examining Board between 1963 and 1971; the present Secretary to the Associated Examining Board, H. O. Childs, for permission to reproduce papers written by the authors in connection with the World History Project sponsored by the board; the members of the World History Project Working Party; Miss J. Street, Miss M. E. Sharland and Mrs. M. A. Emery for deciphering and typing many drafts of the manuscript.

Introduction

The argument put forward and expanded in this book draws upon the developments at the secondary level that have taken place in Britain over the last decade in the two fields of curriculum development and assessment techniques. Although at times developments in these two fields have occurred in parallel this has often been accidental rather than deliberate, and in general there have been far too few points of contact between them, and far too little joint activity. This separation has produced a jerky pattern of advancement with assessment in the main lagging behind curriculum development. Curriculum development is, of course, a complex activity and the experience of recent years has underlined the point that any work in this area will be a barren exercise unless it takes account of such things as teacher attitudes, teaching strategies, materials, staffing needs and organizational patterns. It will also be a barren exercise if no systematic attempt is made to evaluate the courses which give a curriculum its flesh and blood and to use the evidence of such evaluation to modify and change. At the secondary level evaluation of courses and then of the curriculum itself has tended in the past to be undertaken in two main ways. Firstly by teachers in an informal, rather intermittent fashion and secondly through external examinations, mainly of a terminal nature. Neither of these is particularly effective on its own. The first, arising as it does out of teachers' unaided efforts, tends to lack rigour and definition. In consequence it fails to provide as much relevant information as it should. The second has made far too little use of teachers and as a result the assessment provided often fails to match up to the aims of the curriculum. A terminal assessment, moreover, casts a long shadow backwards and can dictate what is taught. What is needed is a co-operative effort between teachers and examining boards, and this is the central theme of this book.

The two authors work in the fields of curriculum development and examinations. In the mid 1960s one (L. A. S.) was co-directing a curriculum laboratory (Goldsmiths') which was to exercise a very significant influence upon the development of inter-disciplinary curricula, and the other (H. G. M.) was Deputy Secretary of a G.C.E. Examining Board, The Associated Examining Board (A.E.B.). In 1967, as a result of looking from two different standpoints at the practical problems facing secondary schools wishing to introduce examinable inter-disciplinary courses, the two authors came together. This book is an account of the results of this partnership and of the activities and colleagues in which and with whom they were associated. The partnership began as a purely pragmatic look at a practical problem but subsequently developed into an attempt to see whether the existing structure of public examinations at the secondary level could be used to promote curriculum development by providing help for those who wished to undertake it.

It is the authors' contention that teachers can exploit the hitherto neglected potential of the existing examination system to provide more appropriate evaluation than in the past. In this way they can aid course development and hence the emergence of a freer curriculum, the term used in this book for curriculum which is directly related to the expressed needs of school.

It may be asked why the authors decided to work within the system and did not instead advocate its abolition. The answer to this lies in the developments that have taken place in external examinations in the past decade which now make it possible for teachers to harness the system if they wish rather than be harnessed to it. As the second chapter shows, criticism has been singularly unsuccessful in getting rid of examinations although a great deal has been done recently to improve them. In such circumstances there seemed to be greater advantages and more likelihood of positive achievement within the system than outside it. This would apply not only to the present national pattern of examinations at the secondary level but to any pattern which might replace it in the future.

The first two chapters describe the position of curriculum development and assessment practice at the secondary level in 1973 as the authors see it. In the light of this picture consideration is then given to the kinds of difficulty which teachers wishing to promote innovation might expect to face. Pointers to possible solutions for some of these difficulties were suggested to the authors by attempts to undertake the assessment of Interdisciplinary Enquiry (I.D.E.), by the development of assessment for an integrated course submitted by the Hedley Walter School, Brentwood, to the A.E.B., and by work done by the A.E.B. between 1967 and 1972 on the assessment of History at 'O' Level. In particular the A.E.B. World History Project seemed to provide a possible model for co-operative innovation in the curriculum through the medium of a public examination.

The lessons learnt from this work are then expanded into a more general statement of the requirements thought to be necessary for developing courses and curriculum in this way, keeping in mind always the situation outlined in the opening chapters. Throughout the keynotes are collaboration and co-operation. Primarily this will involve teachers and examining boards but it must also include all those agencies who have the potential to create an environment within which such co-operation can flourish, for example, Colleges of Education, Universities, Teachers' Centres, L.E.A.s and their staffs.

CHAPTER ONE

Curriculum Development

The emphasis in the past decade upon funded large scale curriculum projects and the proliferation of teaching materials of all kinds make it all too easy to think of curriculum development as a new creation rather than as a continuous process. Looked at in one way, curriculum development is obviously as old as education itself; but for the purposes of this book it is sufficient for us to present an outline of the developments which have taken place within the past twenty years—a period during which the pace of innovation in education has undoubtedly speeded up. In broad terms, this twenty year period of activity divides conveniently into two periods: up to about 1960 and from about 1960 onwards. We shall present our survey within the frame provided by these two periods recognizing, of course, the continuous nature of curriculum development to which reference has already been made.

Up to about 1960

The impetus to curriculum development during this period, like the succeeding years, came originally from developments in primary education whose steady progress over a period of forty years had thrust it into a position which earned justifiable praise both at home and abroad. It was not until the early 1950s, however, that many secondary schools could claim that they were making as much progress as their 'feeders'. Then came a marked surge of exciting developments in secondary education, particularly in the relatively new secondary modern schools.

The success of the secondary modern school is now part of educational history. Most of the developments that took place in these schools in the field of curricula were homespun and this is of tremendous significance. Despite the growth of visual aids and published material, the curriculum of a typical secondary modern school in the mid 1950s stemmed essentially from the efforts and enthusiasm of teachers, who, through flexible programmes designed to develop skills and encourage enquiry, produced a sustained interest from a wide variety of pupils and opened up the rather formal curriculum of earlier years. The outward looking school that received encouragement from the Newsom Report *Half Our Future* was a product of this period of development, and although such schools were nowhere a universal feature of secondary education, there were enough of them scattered around the country to be both noticeable and influential in sponsoring and encouraging developments in other schools. Of course there were 'sour' parts, even in schools that were doing stimulating and worthwhile work within the framework of their home-made programmes. Not all students, even in the best secondary modern schools, enjoyed the fruits of progress on equal terms with their peers. The heated debate over streaming and non-streaming brought this to light and showed that development in the non-selective area, while rapid, was also patchy.

Similarly, the introduction of the extended course which encouraged an ever increasing number of students to stay on at school for an extra year had bad as well as good features. On the one hand such courses brought innumerable benefits to those schools which accepted the challenge to identify and cater for the needs of this older age group. On the other hand they tended to create tensions and divisions within a single school, since the General Certificate of Education (G.C.E.) as the prestigious national secondary examination came to be embraced as a goal for many of these courses, often taken by very small numbers. An external examination thus came to determine not only the nature and content of the courses, but also the direction of much of the work of the school. The value of examinations as a stimulus towards improved standards and the influence that they could exercise upon curriculum were thus in potential conflict and tugged in different directions rather than pulling in the same. Not all teachers, however, who felt the need for an examination external to the school, considered the G.C.E. to be appropriate for their purposes, and the decade 1954–64 saw the establishment of a large number of local school certificates. With these the tug between curriculum and assessment was less apparent. Moreover, the G.C.E. structure did not remain unaltered, and it was largely to meet this new extension of entry that in 1953 an additional G.C.E. Board, the Associated Examining Board, was set up.

A report prepared by J. Vincent Chapman, Secretary of the College of Preceptors, entitled *Your Secondary Modern Schools*, revealed the nature of the developments which were taking place in the field of curriculum in these schools during this pre–1960 period. Although much of the work being done involved developments within subjects, an opening up of the curriculum occurred through the use of various forms of optional programmes taken by students as additions to a core of subjects. There was also a relatively powerful movement towards the integration of subject content within social studies. The feature of these developments which stands out in stark relief is the relative lack of contact between the teachers concerned. Of course, teachers met and discussed mutual problems during this period, but not in the way that was later to become both possible and fashionable. Vincent Chapman provided an important service by making his survey and publishing his findings with regard to the exciting work that was going on within a large number of relatively isolated secondary modern schools, and a few others followed his example. For those who worked in these schools during this period, however, it was clear that for the bulk of their innovative work they were 'on their own'.

During this same period the secondary selective schools also witnessed internally sponsored developments in curriculum. They were, however, nowhere near as innovatory as those taking place within the non-selective sector, generally taking the form of an increase in the number of subjects from which students could choose in order to make their examination programmes as personally geared as possible rather than the development of new courses as such. There were also some developments in the ways in which subjects were presented to students at all levels of the five, six or seven years of the secondary course. There was some slight transfer of ideas between the selective and non-selective sectors, and in this the A.E.B.'s creation and development was helpful. The traditional autonomy, however, of the British school and the nature of the tripartite system as it developed since the 1944 Education Act, militated against any continuous or significant dialogue.

And yet a movement of considerable importance was gradually emerging. Action being taken by teachers, especially in the closing years of the 1950s, was making itself felt, and it was almost as if education was 'girding its loins' in preparation for a massive programme of change. There were many voices calling for change and as many suggestions as to where change might start and where it might lead. It was from within this ferment of educational thinking that the large scale innovations of the post-1960 period found life.

From about 1960

A series of factors combined to produce the large scale curriculum innovation that has been an important part of educational development in Britain during the 1960s and 1970s; but it would be a mistake to draw from the local nature of these factors that such developments were unique to this country. The instrument of change in both Britain and in the United States was the 'curriculum project' and the first subject areas involved in both countries were the sciences and mathematics. In the United States the National Science Foundation provided most of the funding on behalf of the state working through the professional associations, while in Britain the bulk of the funding came initially from the Nuffield Foundation.

As in the United States, in Britain (or more accurately England and Wales) the impetus for subsequent developments at the secondary level came from a variety of sources both inside and outside the school system. Four events in the 1960s were of particular significance here. First the Newsom Report of 1963; secondly the creation of the Certificate of Secondary Education (C.S.E.) in 1964 following the Beloe Report; thirdly the announcement in 1964 by the Labour government of its intention to raise the school leaving age in 1969; and fourthly, in the summer of 1965 the publication by the same government of Circular 10/65 which required all L.E.A.s in England and Wales to prepare plans for comprehensive school reorganization at the secondary level. The influence of all these factors and the developments that resulted from them, will be discussed later in this chapter. Before doing this, however, consideration will be given to the concept of the 'curriculum project' which has proved to be so important to the developments in educational thinking and curriculum change since 1960.

As has already been stated, the curriculum project emerged in both Britain and the United States initially to meet demands for changes within the teaching programmes for both the sciences and mathematics. It is worth devoting space to some of the underlying principles of the project 'model' for two main reasons: firstly, because the pattern established by the original Nuffield science projects has been in large measure adopted by most of the subsequent projects initiated by the Schools Council and, secondly, because no systematic evaluation or critique of the 'project' as a vehicle of curriculum innovation and dissemination in Britain has yet been undertaken. The Schools Council Research Studies Series No 3 *Patterns and Variation in Curriculum Development Projects* has certainly considered differences of approach as between certain projects but it has treated the topic descriptively rather than analytically. The recent £66,000 Ford Foundation grant to the University of East Anglia for research into the effects of curriculum development projects and discovery-based learning, suggests, however, that this omission is to be rectified. The outcome of this work will be of considerable interest and could have repercussions outside as well as inside this country.

In general, British curriculum projects have concentrated upon a particular level of education, mainly the secondary level, and upon traditional subjects. These projects have tended to take as their starting point the relevance or suitability of particular content for students studying the subject at the relevant level and have then embarked on developing materials to meet the identified needs. In the United States the major emphasis has tended to be upon student materials with guides for teachers on how to use them, it being assumed that any teacher upon reading the material could at the drop of a hat develop the relevant teaching strategies to achieve the desired outcomes. In Britain there has been more emphasis upon teacher materials; the teachers thus being made the centre of the instructional process rather than the materials.

Both these approaches raise some significant questions, for example:

1 Should content be the starting point, or should one instead first concentrate upon the student and try to find out to what extent an area of the curriculum can contribute to student growth and development?

2 Should not more emphasis be placed upon the instructional process? (Changing the inputs of instruction may not necessarily change its process.)

Questions such as these would suggest that the traditional approach of most projects to curriculum development, namely, aims, materials, evaluation and teacher education—in that order—is not necessarily the most appropriate. Teachers too often do not take part in the direct development of the materials and are themselves evaluated rather than being the evaluators. How many projects have, for example, developed a resource centre not only for materials but also for suggested instructional techniques to meet specified targets? How many projects have devoted as much time and energy to producing instruments of evaluation as they have to the production of materials? How many projects have concerned themselves with teacher education in the use of existing materials rather than in the development of new ones? The answers to all these questions are the same: 'very few'. Further, even when a project can claim to have undertaken developments on the lines suggested by these questions, the tendency has been for them to have been peripheral to its main activities. This has been particularly true of evaluation, an aspect of which has often been public examinations. As this book will try to show, much more effective use could be made of the examining system but this does not of itself provide the kind of multi-purpose evaluation that new curricula deserve and demand. It needs also to be clearly understood that the assumption that curriculum development is a sequential process involving in turn statement of objectives, development of material to achieve objectives and evaluation to see whether and to what extent these objectives have been achieved is misleading. It is misleading because it is far too simple and because it implies that one stage is separate from the next, or rather that one stage has to be completed before the next can be started. The realities of the situation ensure that these stages constantly interact and interlock. For example, objectives are modified as materials are developed—some disappear, some become more important. The suitability and effectiveness of materials and teaching strategies will, moreover, vary with both teacher and student. The best curriculum development must in a sense be always in a state of flux.

Whatever reservations one may have about the project model, there is no doubt that the very extensive curriculum development programme which has emerged in Britain since 1960 has had a profound effect both upon what is taught in schools and how it is taught. This impact has been mainly, though not exclusively, upon secondary schools.

The Nuffield Foundation's development projects in science were started in 1962. The reforms which they initiated emerged from a movement among practising teachers of science who banded together in the Association for Science Education (A.S.E.). In 1957 a policy statement by the A.S.E. set out proposals for the place of science in the whole system of education. Following this statement reports of groups concerned with teaching methods and syllabuses for biology, chemistry and physics were prepared and it was these that formed the basis of the initial Nuffield Projects. The so-called Nuffield approach was based on two major premises:

1 That Science hitherto taught in a rather rigid fashion which placed the major emphasis upon memorization should be presented to students as a process of enquiry;
2 That ideas presented to the students and the materials used in the classroom should reflect the current thinking of scientists within the relevant area of science modified for the level of the students concerned.

In addition to the science projects, the Nuffield Foundation, in the period 1962–7, was also responsible for funding projects at various levels in the following areas: junior mathematics, modern language teaching, linguistics and English teaching, classics and humanities. These last two were set up jointly with the newly formed Schools Council. The Nuffield Foundation took a further initiative in 1966 when it established the Resources for Learning Project to study ways in which work could be organized in schools in order to make the best possible use of teachers' skills and of new developments in methods and equipment. With the establishment in 1964 of the Schools Council for the Curriculum and Examinations in place of the Secondary Schools Examination Council (a significant change of title) and its increasing involvement in curriculum development, the Nuffield Foundation gradually reduced its work in the area of the school curriculum. The Science Teaching Project, the umbrella under which the original 'O' and 'A' level Projects had developed, became part of the Centre for Science Education at Chelsea College, University of London, the School Classics, the Humanities and the Linguistic and English Teaching Projects were taken over by the Schools Council which also funded an extension of the Modern Languages Project to cover the 13-16 age-group. The Junior Mathematics Project became incorporated as a part of the overall Schools Council curriculum programme in this area while the Resources for Learning Project came to an end in 1972.

The relationship between the Nuffield Foundation's pioneering work in curriculum development and the start and development of the Schools Council's programme of activities is clearly seen as an operational force in the mid-1960s. Since its establishment, the Schools Council has funded more than one hundred and fifty curriculum projects. The majority of these are or were at the secondary level covering the major areas of the curriculum in current use in schools as well as in some areas of experimental development both in content and in the approach to teaching, such as the humanities and the environment. A full list of these projects is published annually by the Schools Council. Each project is funded in the main for periods of three to five years and is based within an existing institution, usually the place of work of the project director, with a small permanent staff seconded from their existing employment.

The Nuffield Foundation programme and the Schools Council's on-going programme for curriculum development have both emphasized the centralizing tendency in 'curriculum-thinking' in Britain, in spite of the fact that teachers have been involved either as members of project teams or in the trial of materials in their schools. This involvement has, however, been comparatively small in terms of numbers as well as being comparatively selective. This has resulted in most teachers being introduced to curriculum innovation at second hand in the capacity of 'shoppers' in the ever-growing materials market. The North West Regional Curriculum Project, sponsored by the Schools Council initially in 1967, is, however, a notable exception to this generalization and has had very considerable contact with teachers in the creation of materials. The evaluation of its worth is thus likely to provide important information on the question of teacher involvement in sponsored curriculum development.

Secondary school teachers at the classroom level were, however, presented with a golden opportunity to make their own massive contribution to curriculum development at least within the 14-16 age-range when the Certificate of Secondary Education first mooted by the Beloe Report was later developed as a practical examination system by fourteen regional examination boards in 1964-6. The developments of this particular examination are dealt with more fully in Chapter 2, but it can be said here that in terms of curriculum development the initial outpourings of the many subject panels of specially chosen teachers in the fourteen regions of England and Wales were, in the main, very familiar to many of those who would subsequently be involved in turning them into programmes of

educational activity and assessment in their own schools. An opportunity
to take giant strides in developing curriculum for the 14–16 age-group
was missed. There were, however, mitigating circumstances, not the least
being the decision to establish an equivalence between Grade 1 in C.S.E.
and an 'O' level pass. No critic, therefore, of the work undertaken in
great haste by the teachers involved could reasonably expect giant strides
to be made during this period. Perhaps the greatest long-term benefit of
this work arose from the opportunity it provided for teachers from secondary schools scattered over relatively wide areas to come together and
discuss the teaching of their subjects. This was not a new event by any
means, but the frequency of the meetings of these same teachers in their
small groups and the widespread nature of the calls-to-meeting which
came not only from the fourteen regional boards but also from the smaller
Advisory or Local Consortia Groups were immensely beneficial. The
experience enjoyed by these teachers and those involved in the Nuffield,
Schools Council and other projects left its mark, and with the emergence
of teachers' centres in large numbers the opportunity was provided for a
continuation of fruitful discussion over a whole range of educational
activities. What was significant about these discussions was that they were
no longer confined to the relative isolation of the school staff room. The
comparative informality of teachers' centres also helped a great deal and
ensured that small group discussions replaced to a large extent the set
piece lecture as the central feature of 'in-service education'. In the long
run, curriculum development in this country will owe a great debt to the
greater ease with which teachers can, if they wish, meet and discuss in this
way.

The force of this point is to be seen from the outcome of small group
meetings which took place in many parts of the country as a result of the
declaration of intent to raise the school leaving age. Some RoSLA working
parties set up in the main by the administrative and advisory staff of local
education authorities made a considerable contribution to evaluation based
upon practical experience of alternatives to the existing secondary school
curriculum patterns. Indeed, a few added to these patterns; for example,
the working party at Eastleigh which in 1966–7 took a global view of the
curriculum at this level, recognizing that programmes for older students
must have their beginnings in the earlier years of schooling. The fate,
however, of the declaration of intent to raise the school leaving age in
1969 and its subsequent postponement tended to dampen much of the
enthusiasm that had been generated in many areas. In consequence the
decision taken in May 1972 to raise the school leaving age as from September 1972 failed to create the same stir that the original announcement had
made. This is not to say that RoSLA was not an important trigger to curri-

culum development. The educational needs of the 16 year old group crops up time and time again in the projects mounted by the Schools Council although it should be added that these Projects have been concerned with the whole of the 5 to 19 year age range.

The pros and cons of a comprehensive schooling have been long debated in this country, and Circular 10/65 only added heat and urgency to these debates. Although the notion of comprehensive education forms a power-ful basis for curriculum thinking and will no doubt become increasingly important in this respect as the years pass, it has not so far produced a great deal in practice except in those areas where special efforts have been made to develop programmes for comprehensive schools no matter how organ-ized. Examples of such efforts include the work done by L.E.A. sponsored working parties established in Leicestershire, Oxfordshire and Shropshire and more recently in Nottinghamshire and Hampshire. It seems pertinent to state that in these areas the problems associated with comprehensive organization of middle and secondary education have been tackled with L.E.A. backing and by teachers who are actively engaged in the schools concerned. Like the RoSLA programmes of the late 1960s, these pro-grammes of comprehensive education are adding weight to teacher-sponsored curriculum for their own students.

In this brief review of curriculum development since 1950, mention should be made of two completely different projects which have had a significant impact on work in schools. Surprisingly, particularly when contrasted with the large scale projects mentioned earlier in this chapter, both of these have emerged from the work of two very small groups of teachers; the first of these is the School Mathematics Project (S.M.P.) and the second the Fourfold Curriculum developed by the Curriculum Laboratory at University of London Goldsmiths' College.

The School Mathematics Project, despite making use of the project model, being national in scope and influence and concerned with the pro-duction of classroom materials, differed, in some respects quite markedly, from other major curriculum projects established in Britain. Although most British projects, in contrast to those in the United States, have been small in terms of their central staffing and funding, the S.M.P. was (and indeed is) small to a peculiar degree. It started, as Bryan Thwaites describes in his account of its first ten years, with a meeting in 1961 in a Winchester garden between himself and the senior mathematics masters of three lead-ing independent schools. This small group together with one other school agreed to co-operate in the planning of a radically new mathematics syllabus, to devise a new G.C.E. examination for assessing this syllabus and to provide suitable textbooks. Ten years later all of this and more had been achieved, and it is estimated that by 1972 over half the secondary schools in England were using S.M.P. materials. They have also been used extensively overseas. Yet this achievement took place without national funding, without official support and with minimal central staff and support services. As Dr Harrison in his view of 'S.M.P. The First Ten Years' in *Education* (9 February 1973) rightly points out, one of the most important and satisfying features of S.M.P. was the extent to which it was teacher-based. This substantial teacher involvement was, moreover, carried out within what is still a remarkably informal administrative structure. The nature and extent of this involvement has made S.M.P. much more successful than most projects in the dissemination process and in the prolongation of useful life which is so critical if a project is to have any lasting influence upon the curriculum. Too often, six or so years after a curriculum project has burst upon the educational scene, all that is left is a heap of expensively produced books and materials available for purchase in the local bookshop.

It is interesting to note two other features of S.M.P. both of which are shared with the Nuffield and Schools Council Projects, particularly the former, although to a different degree. The first is the extent to which the independent schools were involved. The early work of S.M.P. and the Nuffield Science Projects owed much to the professionalism, hard work and enthusiasm of those in senior positions in independent schools and to the willingness of the heads of these same schools to release their best staff upon secondment. The second is the way in which public examinations, in this case the G.C.E., became involved in the projects. In the case of the S.M.P. this was built in from the beginning; with the earlier Nuffield projects, G.C.E., as it were, came in by the side door when it was appreciated that students prepared upon the 'new approach' and using the 'new materials' would be assessed upon an 'old' examination.

This involvement of the G.C.E. had important repercussions which are referred to again in the second chapter. It first of all led to a much closer co-operation between the examining boards since it was decided that one G.C.E. examining board should undertake the administration of a project examination on behalf of the others. This had two advantages; first that in the long run it spread the cost of the administrative load more evenly among the boards and secondly that as project examinations increased it widened the opportunities for boards to participate in experimental work. The requirements of the new curricula meant that new approaches were necessary to assess them. The Nuffield projects in particular were thus an important element in the wave of developmental work undertaken by G.C.E. boards, especially after 1966. Unfortunately, this same degree of co-operation is only just beginning to be shown by the C.S.E. boards in relation to those national projects which have been concerned with a wider ability range or with the less able such as Secondary Science and the Schools Council's Modern Language Projects. A golden opportunity of avoiding duplication of effort and engaging economically in development work upon common problems of assessment has thus been lost.

The nature and timing of the involvement of the G.C.E. boards in the examining of projects has, however, left something to be desired. All too often those concerned with the examining of projects have been called in after the objectives have been determined and ossification has already started to set in. The opportunity for experimentation in the period before a final examination whose results count has to be devised has thus been lost. This situation, which has regrettably been a feature of nearly all projects involving national examinations, the Schools Council Integrated Science Project being a notable exception, has limited the amount of evaluation undertaken upon the project, and has on occasion meant that the actual examination itself has not fully met expectations. Moreover, the use of an externally recognized examination in this way can itself contribute to inflexibility. The time needed to amend examinations and the importance of providing proper notice of change can easily set a pattern in a situation where it is not entirely desirable to do so. Despite these deficiencies, however, the involvement of examining boards in the assessment of national projects has provided a significant pointer to the future. It was certainly a key feature of the work done at the outset by those involved in the creation of the second unique 'project' we wish to describe and which had its beginnings at University of London Goldsmiths' College in 1964.

In that year, the Department of Education and Science asked Goldsmiths' to mount 'pilot' in-serivce courses for senior experienced teachers from secondary schools who were 'to study the ways and means teachers could implement the findings of the Newsom Report *Half Our Future* which had been published a year earlier'. The first pilot course was started in January 1965 under the tutorship of Charity James; and the twenty-seven head-teachers and senior staff who were seconded for a term's participation on the course decided to tackle their brief in ways which nobody could have foreseen. After a pause of a term, the second pilot course started in September 1965 under the tutorship of Charity James, Edwin Mason and Professor Florence Roane (from Florida, U.S.A.). The twenty-four participants (one of whom was Leslie Smith) agreed very speedily to reject the D.E.S.'s brief and instead to concentrate upon the creation of a new curriculum for secondary education, building on the work done by the first pilot course and by the numerous schools which were involved. Within ten very full weeks of intense activity at Goldsmiths' College, the second pilot course for experienced teachers emerged with a basis for a 'completely new' approach to education which involved, among other things, the notion of Inter-disciplinary Enquiry (I.D.E.) and a new view of the notion of assessment of on-going work in school. As had happened after the first course, the participants of the second course returned to their schools to initiate or continue radical programmes of renewal of their curricula, their educational approaches, and of their assessment procedures. Within weeks it was made clear to the small team at Goldsmiths' that a supportive agency was needed to assist these schools with their development work; and by the time the third pilot course had concluded its study of socially handicapped students, this supportive agency—the Curriculum Laboratory—had been founded by Charity James, Edwin Mason and Leslie Smith. It was this small team, working closely with a number of schools, that devised the Fourfold Curriculum which, when published within reports and the magazine *Ideas*, was to cause a stir in educational circles not only in Britain but in many parts of the world.

Some references will be made to the nature of the Fourfold Curriculum later in this book, but of interest at this point is the initiative taken by one of the authors (L.A.S.) to launch a group-based study of the problems of assessment which would enable the new curriculum to be applied within the later years of secondary education (as well as earlier and after) and submitted for external certification by both G.C.E. and C.S.E. examining boards. The results of this effort to bring in the external examinations system at the outset of a 'movement', which involved schools in the interpretation of their own views of the Fourfold Curriculum, are reported in Chapter Three. Of importance in this chapter devoted to curriculum development is a note to the effect that the work of the Curriculum Laboratory quickly assumed an importance nationally, not because hundreds of schools started to adopt it as their own curriculum, but because it represented a 'new look' which became more clearly articulated as the years passed. It thus became a 'point of reference' in the dialogue of the time and is still an influential force in educational practice.

And so we come to 1973. It would serve no useful purpose to describe in detail here the numerous projects that have been launched in the past decade or which await their beginning, projects which (as has already been stressed) together constitute the largest, most varied, most expensive and most complex programme of curriculum development ever undertaken in England and Wales. Instead, attention will be drawn to five features of recent curriculum innovation, none of them new, which in combination serve to present a brief description of the major elements in the secondary curriculum of 1973.

The first and perhaps the most powerful is 'enquiry based learning'. The Nuffield Projects, most of the Schools Council sponsored projects and the many approaches to curriculum development introduced by other agencies such as the Goldsmiths' Curriculum Laboratory, all make enquiry based learning central to their programmes for students of all ages and their teachers. Although there is still a long road to travel before the potential of enquiry based learning is fully realized, it is better understood today than it was ten years ago. There are, of course, many meanings to the term, and in the classroom much goes on in its name without adding much to the educational development of those involved. This should not, how-ever, cause us to underrate its importance as a concept but rather make us look critically at the techniques of applying it in practice.

Another term that has been with us for many years is 'integration', and this also figures prominently in present day curriculum literature and dis-cussion. This approach to education needs a great deal of attention from the point of view of our understanding of its practical applications. In other parts of the world, particularly in Australasia, integration is often referred to as 'correlation'. The bringing together of segments from selected sub-jects, which this latter term implies, was a feature of the 1950s brand of social studies and still goes on today in much so-called integrated activity. On the other hand there are examples of 'integrated studies' or activities which do not follow this pattern and which offer instead an exciting view of curriculum development which spans the humanities, applied sciences, technology, arts and crafts and the expressive arts on their own or in combination. At the present time, 'integrated' studies in this latter sense are enjoying an upswing. It is likely, moreover, that they will sustain their position largely because the rationale for their inclusion in the school curriculum has been more effectively argued than heretofore and because those undertaking such courses have become more effective in achieving their aims.

'Inter-disciplinary enquiry' and 'intra-disciplinary enquiry' are two further features of modern curriculum development which have an im-portant place in this work. They came together as two of the elements of the Fourfold Curriculum developed by the Curriculum Laboratory at Goldsmiths' although the notion of intra-disciplinary enquiry is very old indeed. Both of these features draw heavily on the enquiry based approach, albeit in a very sophisticated fashion. Also, both can be looked upon, according to one's viewpoint, as a reaction against or a development from integrated studies. In practice inter-disciplinary enquiry very often re-sembles integrated studies, and intra-disciplinary enquiry can be seen as specialist subject teaching. As parts, however, of a global approach to the curriculum of the secondary and middle school, they can represent some-thing new and different.

Finally, there is the term 'process'. All of the other four features mentioned make play with this aspect of teaching and learning. It is an extremely difficult concept to pin down and apply within educational activity largely due to the loose way it is used in discussion. It is hoped that this book will help in this respect.

It would be a mistake to assume that these five features, part of the jargon of those engaged in curriculum development and not often clearly defined, are necessarily descriptive of educational activity in the majority of schools. While we know that this is not the case, there is no doubt that the educational environment is being very substantially affected by them. They may represent activities which individual staff members of schools may choose not to adopt, but the time is now passing when such decisions result from a failure to consider or simply from ignorance; instead they are the outcome of increasingly informed discussion. There is, moreover, a growing tendency for innovation to be introduced step by step so that when it finally comes it ceases for those involved to be innovation. There is thus infinite variety of active discussion, active involvement and active use, all of which make a move towards a freer curriculum (here implying the loosening of constraints) easier to achieve. The constraint with which this book is particularly concerned is that of external examinations and its main purpose is to suggest that all the five features of curriculum development mentioned above can be catered for within the existing examination framework.

It must also be remembered that although new developments in curriculum for the secondary school have probably been greater in the past decade than ever before, the staple diet of the majority of students still remains the acquisition of skills and knowledge within a single disciplinary or subject based curriculum. This, therefore, must be the starting point of any discussion. In 1973 such a curriculum in a co-educational school probably includes as its core the following: English (involving both language and literature), mathematics, science(s), history, geography, religious studies, foreign languages, music, art and light crafts, woodwork, metalwork, technical drawing, home economics, needlecraft and physical education. There are, of course, infinite variations to this basic core curriculum to meet the particular needs of individual schools or to harness the talents of particular teachers. Increasingly in recent years, courses such as social studies, business studies, engineering, civic education or government and, less frequently, economics and sociology are found as part of the core.

With the exception of the subjects mentioned towards the end of the previous paragraph, those listed represent a view of the curriculum which has changed but little in subject terms over the past twenty years or more. The mere listing of subjects, however, tells us nothing about extensive development work which has taken place recently within subject boundaries and has resulted in considerable changes both in content and in teaching strategies. Any move towards a 'freer' curriculum, therefore, must take account of a rapidly developing conventionally subject based curriculum as well as of innovations of the kind described earlier in this chapter. The word 'must' has been used advisedly since much of the opposition to innovation has taken place 'inside' subjects. By opposition in this context one means not only opposition within the teaching profession but also among parents and employers. A subject based approach is also important in relation to assessment since it is necessary to solve or provide possible solutions for the assessment of new approaches within existing subjects before tackling the more complex assessment problems created by the development of an integrated curriculum.

A subject based approach must not, however, cause us to neglect the potential for integration that lies within many subjects—history being a notable example—nor should it cause us to underrate the pressures to which the traditional curriculum is at present being subjected. Many new or relatively new areas of concern are pressing their case for inclusion in the secondary school curriculum; for example, health education, careers education, politics, anthropology, environmental studies, consumer education and computer science (the list is far from exhaustive). Pressure here is both in relation to status as subjects in their own right and as part of newly designed integrated or inter-disciplinary courses. The same is true of acitivities and studies like design, technology and a host of craft activities which are growing beyond the stage of being offered to students as partially developed options.

Enough has been said to suggest that the curriculum in secondary schools. whatever one's standpoint in relation to integrated work, is in a fluid expanding state with all the associated excitement and confusion that such a situation brings with it. To talk of the curriculum purely in the context of subjects as has been done over the last few paragraphs is, moreover, quite misleading. Any curriculum development must involve a re-thinking of attitudes by both teacher and student. This is in its turn but a part, albeit a crucial one, of the total environment with which anything new has eventually to come to terms. In the case of the curriculum this must involve such things as the design of the school itself and the nature and extent of the resources available. At the secondary level in particular, it must also involve those who subsequently employ the products of the schools and this inevitably implies assessment and evaluation.

In the past, examinations have been viewed as imposing constraints upon a far more rigid subject based curriculum than even the most conservative would suggest as being relevant today for the 15–19 year old age range in secondary and further education. Its potential as a constraint in

the future would seem, therefore, to be much greater. Recent developments in the examination system have, however, provided opportunities
to ensure that this need not be the case. These developments will be discussed in the next chapter as a prelude to a consideration of what difficulties
still exist and what bottlenecks require identification and removal. Until
this is done the potential in the system cannot be exploited to the maximum
advantage.

CHAPTER TWO

Assessment Development

One of the most common and abiding criticisms of the external examination system at the secondary level in England and Wales is that it inhibits curriculum development because it exercises a deadening influence upon the courses which exemplify the curriculum in action. The curriculum (critics say) is what the examining boards print in their syllabuses, and in consequence it is all too often unrelated to the real needs of schools. In view of this it is perhaps surprising that those wishing to introduce a new curriculum and hence to develop new courses at the secondary level (whose numbers in recent years at least have been large) have been able in practice to achieve very little reduction in the influence of external examinations and have been singularly unsuccessful in securing their abolition. Possible reasons for this are worth considering in rather more detail.

In the period prior to 1950 criticisms, while voiced, were not sustained with any real conviction since those who sat for external examinations at secondary schools came from a relatively small homogeneous group who required certification for a comparatively limited range of purposes. In consequence it was not difficult to establish a consensus among those involved as to what were appropriate courses of study, and this situation was reflected in the examinations provided. Since that time great changes have taken place. The homogeneous pattern of entry has disappeared. The numbers staying on at school and taking external examinations have vastly increased, particularly since 1960, and in consequence so has the use made of external certification. In such circumstances it became virtually impossible to establish a consensus about appropriate curriculum patterns. It was not surprising therefore that criticism of external examining boards increased in the early 1960s and accelerated rapidly thereafter as new developments in the curriculum took place. This criticism was less severe than it might have been because the earliest post-war curriculum developments epitomized by the Nuffield Sciences and the School Mathematics Project took place within orthodox subject based disciplines and were concerned to a greater extent with content, materials, skills and teaching methods than with the nature of the secondary school curriculum itself. The G.C.E. examining boards, which were then expanding in size to meet the greatly increased entry, were thus able to meet the needs of a majority of their schools and to satisfy a teaching profession for whom external examinations were in the main feather beds rather than beds of nails. In order to do so, however, they had to investigate new approaches to assessment and to embark on substantial development work.

The utility, moreover, of external examinations for a society which still placed great store by policies designed to select or admit the few, and for schools who desired to have a yardstick against which to measure their achievement, blunted much of the criticism. The fact that in Britain there was no national examining board but several different approved examining boards functioning side by side also permitted some variety. This variety was further increased by the creation in 1953 of the Associated Examining Board.

The A.E.B., which conducted examinations for the first time in 1955, differed from the other G.C.E. Boards in that it was not directly associated with a particular university or group of universities. Even allowing for the very substantial increase in G.C.E. entries as a whole which affected all boards in the 1960s, the development of the A.E.B. has been impressive and is a tribute to the vision and hard work of those who founded it. (In summer 1955, 2,409 candidates took the A.E.B. examinations at 'O' and 'A' level. In summer 1965 this figure was 102,993, of whom 29,751 came from secondary modern schools. By summer 1972 the A.E.B. entry had increased to 177,164, of whom 38,287 were from secondary modern schools and 35,512 from comprehensive schools. The total number of 'O' and 'A' level candidates nationally for 1955 and 1972 were 243,109 and 879,732.) By the mid 1960s the A.E.B. was beginning to introduce some interesting innovations in both syllabuses and methods of assessment, notably in the social sciences and in modern languages, and as the size and scope of its entry increased so did its influence. The General Certificate of Education, introduced in 1950, helped in this development since its single subject nature, in contrast to the grouped nature of the School and Higher Certificates which it replaced, made it easier, in theory at least, to introduce new subjects into the examination structure and thus to modify the curriculum. Those possibilities were not always realized in practice, however, and for this the subject committees of the Secondary Schools Examinations Council must take a substantial share of the blame.[1] The examining boards also found it difficult to change their traditional roles as administrative bodies which simply provided examinations, and they were not geared in terms of organization and staffing to the furtherance of curriculum innovation.

[1] The Secondary Schools Examinations Council had originally been set up in 1917 by the then Board of Education to co-ordinate the work of the boards who administered the School and Higher Certificate examinations, to maintain standards between the Boards and to approve new syllabuses. In 1950 it took over the same function in relation to the G.C.E. It was replaced in 1964 by the Schools Council for the Curriculum and the Examinations.

The development work referred to earlier began on a sizeable scale as far as most of the G.C.E. boards were concerned in the period 1965–8. The pressure for change came basically from two directions; first from the initial wave of curriculum projects, particularly those in science, and secondly from a desire to improve the quality of the G.C.E. examinations as a whole. The 'Nuffield approach' in science as we have seen in Chapter 1 emphasized enquiry based learning. If this was to be realized in practice, it had to be reflected in both teaching methods and examinations. Unfortunately too little emphasis in these early projects was placed upon defining what was meant by enquiry based learning in terms of the skills needed to achieve it successfully in practice. External examinations moreover came in as an afterthought since assessment and evaluation did not form an integral part of the projects from the outset. As a result some of the earlier examination papers produced by the G.C.E. boards responsible for the work did not altogether match up to the expectations of the teachers and the project organizers. In the preparation of these papers, however, much valuable work was undertaken upon types of question, which led the G.C.E. boards to look seriously for the first time at objective testing, a technique long and extensively used in the United States. A number of boards sent staff to the United States to study American practice and to attend courses on test construction. This contact had important consequences for the development of assessment in England and Wales that extended far beyond the use of objective testing itself as a component of G.C.E. examinations. The American approach to test construction emphasized to a marked degree the technical aspects of testing, an area which at that time had been almost totally neglected in British secondary school examinations. This emphasis gave impetus to the work of a number of individuals within examining boards who were increasingly disturbed by the absence in the G.C.E. of any quality control in a technical sense. One such was the late Mr G. Bruce, Secretary to the University Entrance and Schools Examinations Council, University of London, who, concerned with the problems of a rapidly rising entry, was anxious to introduce objective testing as a component of G.C.E. examinations where it seemed appropriate. This he was successful in doing despite initial opposition. There were also individuals outside the examining board structure in universities and organizations like the National Foundation for Educational Research who were equally concerned, but their practical influence was small since at that time they were unable to involve the examining boards in their work. A notable exception was the School of Education at the University of Manchester which in conjunction with the Joint Matriculation Board initiated work leading to actual rather than theoretical improvements. Some of this work is described in the Joint

Matriculation Boards's series of Occasional Publications which was started in 1954.[1]

The increased use of objective testing also had an immediate practical impact. It led first of all to a far more professional approach to test construction. The design of an objective question (or item as it is more commonly called) lends itself readily to statistical analysis and requires those producing it to weigh every word most carefully. Objective test construction is, moreover, an exercise that can only be undertaken properly by a group and not by individuals. It did not take long for this very different approach to test construction to rub off on to other types of question and to techniques of assessment in general. Secondly, the use of objective tests brought the behavioural objectives approach out of the arena of theory into that of practice in Britain. The arguments against this approach in relation to curriculum development are sufficiently well rehearsed not to require further elaboration.[2] These disadvantages also apply to test construction, but here its influence, despite relatively limited application so far, has been undeniably beneficial.

In the second half of the 1960s, as the first chapter shows, the pace of curriculum development in secondary schools not only accelerated but changed direction and took an increasingly integrated and inter-disciplinary form. This was partly the result of developments within primary schools, partly a by-product of the extension of comprehensive education and partly a result of increased staying on at school beyond the statutory leaving age. For those schools which wished to develop integrated curricula the existing examination structure posed, on the face of it, an insuperable problem. What would have happened had it not been for the opportunity presented by the new Certificate of Secondary Education (C.S.E.) for development and innovation within the existing system is a matter for speculation, but one thing is certain, that without C.S.E. more and more teachers would have advocated the abolition of external examinations.

Why was C.S.E., established in 1964 on the recommendation of the Beloe Report, so significant? Why in retrospect may it turn out to have been for Britain one of the most significant educational events of the twentieth century? The reasons for making these rather sweeping statements are four in number:

1 It involved teachers directly for the first time in assessment in nationally recognized external examinations.

[1] Readers of this chapter will find the following Occasional Publications to be of particular interest, Nos. 12, 13, 19, 22, 25, 26, 27, 30, 31, 32, 33 and 34. Full details are to be found in the bibliography.
[2] An article by D. Hogben in the May 1972 edition of the Journal of Curriculum Studies entitled 'The Behavioural Objectives Approach, Some Problems and Some Dangers' summarizes the arguments admirably. It also contains a useful bilbiography.

2 It took teachers for the first time in substantial numbers into schools other than their own.

3 It stimulated the development and use of a much wider range of techniques of assessment.

4 It introduced the school based or Mode 3 examination.

The fourth point is in reality the culmination of the first point but the two need separate consideration, however artificial at times the distinction between them may become.

C.S.E. thus created an environment for curriculum development and innovation within the national external examination structure.[1] The opportunity was given to teachers to visit other schools to see and criticize constructively what was going on there. Examining boards began to consider in detail the purposes of the assessment they were providing and in consequence to make use of techniques of assessment which they had previously ignored or had decided were only feasible for use with small numbers. In this they were aided by the newly constituted Schools Council. These techniques included amongst others objective testing, projects or individual studies, the use of course work and the continuous assessment of pupil performance. The introduction of such techniques, some of which could only be undertaken if the pupil's own teacher was involved, necessitated the introduction of research and development studies by examining boards and caused them to give thought to the nature and size of their staffs. Teachers became more actively involved in the work of examining boards not only in a representative capacity but in the decision-making process affecting their own pupils. Above all Mode 3 provided a unique opportunity to combine an evaluation of a course of a teacher's own choice, with certification in a nationally recognized external examination. The term Mode 3 was originally introduced with the establishment of C.S.E. in 1964. Although in theory it is available in both C.S.E. and G.C.E. in practice G.C.E. Boards vary very markedly in their attitude to it. In Mode 3 the syllabus and the assessment is proposed by a single school or group of schools who also carry out the grading of the pupils concerned, these grades being moderated by the examining boards. It is necessary to make the point, however, that the term, like so much educational terminology, has become blurred in use. There are, for example, many current Mode 1 or external examinations in which there is a substantial Mode 3 or school-based component.

The opportunity for curriculum development and innovation provided

[1] The word 'national' has been used advisedly here since the strengths of certain of the local school certificates established in the decade before the coming of C.S.E. are often overlooked, for example, those in Reading and Hertfordshire. Their contribution to curriculum development in a local context was often significant.

by C.S.E., is obvious, and yet by early 1973 when this book was being written it had been grasped by very few. In 1972, Mode 3 accounted for only 14.8 per cent of all the subject entries in C.S.E.; the number of approved Mode 3s in G.C.E. at 'O' level was minimal and at 'A' level non-existent. Possibly even more significant is the fact that many Mode 3s are currently being put forward not for educational reasons but for reasons of administrative convenience. In consequence much of the hard work undertaken has not led to any significant improvement in existing curricula or to new developments. Why is this?

There are a number of reasons. First of all there are the difficulties created by the present examination system. The existence side by side of two examinations of 16+, one graded, the other pass/fail, and of two sets of boards with different syllabuses, one set obliged to accept Mode 3 proposals in principle, the other not, does not encourage schools with pupils entering for both examinations to experiment. Moreover the C.S.E. boards differ very markedly in their attitudes to Mode 3 proposals, despite their constitutional position which gives them in theory comparatively limited powers of rejection. Additionally, the development of inter-disciplinary courses for whose assessment Mode 3 is essential has been hindered by the examination pattern adopted in the G.C.E., which reflects the single disciplinary nature of the overwhelming majority of secondary school curricula at the present time. Finally, examining bodies, despite recent changes, are still not able or willing to spend the sums of money necessary to promote research and development into the problems created by school-based assessment and to investigate the range of techniques required. This is particularly true of C.S.E. boards which, in relation to the problems with which they have to deal, are inadequately financed and staffed. Also, it is only fair to make the point that recent developments in methods of examining have led to increased involvement by teachers in both G.C.E. and C.S.E., making the Mode 1 examinations more satisfactory and less open to criticism. It is important too to appreciate that curriculum development ought never to be undertaken at the expense of the pupil. The development of a new course assessed under a Mode 3 arrangement by a single teacher could put pupils seriously at risk if the teacher were to leave in the middle of the course. Heads, rightly concerned to see that this does not happen, may therefore put a brake upon such single-handed developments. This underlines once again the importance of the co-operative group approach to curriculum development.

These are all practical difficulties, and while very real and serious can be solved if the will is there. There are, however, a number of more fundamental issues involved which act as obstacles to curriculum development and innovation through the use of Mode 3. These are much less easy to overcome since their solution requires attitudes to change. There is, first of all, the attitude of teachers to themselves as assessors. Owing to the nature and importance of external examinations in England and Wales a distinction has grown up in the minds of many teachers between assessment as a natural classroom activity and assessment as an external artificial exercise conducted by some outside agency. This distinction is entirely artificial and has caused teachers to neglect assessment as an integral part of their professional work.

This attitude to assessment is reflected in the instruction provided for teachers in this field during their training period. The basic principles of assessment are rarely discussed in any detail, even in 1973, and the opportunities for applying them in practice in pre-service training are almost non-existent. Considerable strides have been made in recent years in relation to in-service training but much remains to be done as the Schools Council have recently publicly recognized in their Examinations Bulletin No. 23. This situation has meant that teachers considering the development of Mode 3 have been held back by their concern over the need to provide appropriate assessment or, even worse, have been providing inappropriate assessment for the courses they have developed.

Secondly, examining boards today, both C.S.E. and G.C.E., still regard themselves in the main, not as educational, but as administrative bodies. They see their role primarily as one of organizing to the best of their ability the examinations that they have and of refining the techniques of assessment they use rather than as one of assisting in curriculum development. Their staffing has been organized accordingly. This negative view of their role assumes that examining can be undertaken as an exercise isolated from the rest of the educational process. It also assumes that taking a positive line in relation to curriculum development must, of necessity, interfere with a school's freedom of action, historically a sacred cow. The necessary marriage between curriculum development as it takes place in schools and assessment as an evaluation instrument developed by examining boards in conjunction with schools has thus never been consummated to the great disadvantage of the curriculum.

Such points must be borne in mind lest one presents too rosy a view of the future. It would be unwise to assume that the majority of teachers or examining boards see the present situation in regard to assessment as containing the potential for future curriculum improvement that the authors have suggested. Moreover, the organizational patterns adopted by schools and their physical layout may well discourage or hinder new developments even when these are desired.

CHAPTER THREE

Curriculum and Assessment Development.
A Personalized Encounter

The first two chapters have described the situation in 1973 in relation to curriculum development and assessment at the secondary level as the authors see it. Possibilities for the future have been suggested and assertions made which some readers will probably think are unrealistic and incapable of achievement in practice. The remaining chapters provide a justification for these assertions. This will be done initially by drawing upon the authors' own experiences. These will subsequently be generalized and a strategy developed in the last two chapters for exploiting the potential for curriculum and course development inherent in the present situation.

The justification for recounting personal experiences here is not that they are typical or unique but that they represent a fusion between two areas of the education service: curriculum development and examination administration, which many still regard as being totally incompatible. The fusion is also one between ideals and practice. These experiences would seem to suggest that teachers wishing to devise their own courses can, without losing any idealism or compromising principles, use to their advantage what the existing external examination system has to offer in terms of evaluation combined with nationally recognized certification.

A major thread running through the past fifteen years for L. A. Smith and for many other teachers has been that of growing integration within the curriculum. This has been particularly significant in the social sciences at the secondary level, although by no means exclusive to this area, or level. In the 1950s integration showed itself in the introduction of a wide variety of social studies courses for pupils up to age 15 and in a resurgence of general science within secondary schools. In the 1960s it was to blossom into rather more sophisticated forms (for example the Fourfold Curriculum at Goldsmiths') and in consequence its potential for influence within schools increased. New integrated courses in science, to which reference has already been made, were developed and the possibilities inherent in areas such as design technology and in themes such as the environment began to be recognized and explored. Social studies courses began to concentrate upon current areas of controversy and to use traditional disciplines as a means of bringing to bear a variety of different perspectives upon a single problem.

At the end of the first chapter the words and phrases 'integration', 'inter-disciplinary enquiry' and 'intra-disciplinary enquiry' were used without any attempt at definition. Failure to define now can only cause confusion. In a dictionary 'integration' is described as 'the act of making a whole out of parts'. It is thus a wide-ranging umbrella term unlike the other two which are more specific and more extreme. One of the major factors stimulating curriculum change in recent years has been the blurring of the boundary lines between subject areas. Links have developed where none were previously thought to exist. This process has taken place both within disciplines—as in the emergence of courses in physical science—and between disciplines—as in the coming together of history and geography under the umbrella of social studies. One of the main problems with the label 'integrated' when attached to courses and curricula is that the degree of integration can vary widely from a systematic attempt to use different disciplines as a means of providing a variety of insights into a common theme to the occasional involvement of a geographer and/or economist in a history course.

The phrases 'inter-' and 'intra-disciplinary enquiry' can be considered together, the key word being enquiry. The creators of the Fourfold Curriculum at Goldsmiths' called enquiry their 'central pillar'. They believed that once enquiry started and an attempt was made to solve fundamental problems then the barriers between disciplines which in the context of the compartmentalized nature of most school curricula had appeared formidable would become largely irrelevant. Work became inter-disciplinary because it was necessary to use a variety of disciplines in order to formulate problems, to draw up hypotheses for solution and to record findings. One might say that the essential difference between integration and inter-disciplinary enquiry is that the former tends rather self-consciously to bring disciplines together in order to merge them, while the latter initiates enquiry naturally from no particular disciplinary standpoint and uses the disciplines as it needs them to help provide answers. Earlier in this paragraph the words 'largely irrelevant' were used in relation to barriers between disciplines. This was done because it is not absolutely necessary that enquiry should be conducted solely in an inter-disciplinary context although it may well be more wide-ranging if it is. It is possible and indeed worthwhile to do so within single disciplines hence the term 'intra-disciplinary enquiry'. These ideas were originally described in *The Raising of the School Leaving Age*, the report of the Second Pilot Course for Experienced Teachers, University of London, Goldsmiths' College.

B

These developments have raised a host of fundamental questions. Some are philosophical, for example, what makes a particular discipline unique, or, put in another way, do disciplines have underlying structures which are unique to themselves? Others are severely practical, for example: is the teaching of integrated courses best undertaken by specialists or generalists? What teaching strategies and organizational structures within schools are best suited for the development of integrated courses, and how might teachers set about developing new courses in areas of the curriculum where little or no help is available from past experience.

At this stage an important general point should be made about the development of integrated courses in secondary schools over the past fifteen years. Despite the conceptual demands of such courses, which are probably greater than those made by courses based upon single disciplines, they have been rarely developed for the full ability range. Indeed the reverse has usually been the case, and they have been introduced, initially at least, for the less able. Until the coming of C.S.E., moreover, they very often did not extend beyond the fourth year. This has meant that pupils in the sixth form have been little exposed to inter-disciplinary work.

The sixth form pattern has been almost exlusively academic. The prospects there for new developments of an integrated nature and of more varied patterns of assessment have not been encouraging. In consequence this chapter, and indeed the book as a whole, concentrate on curriculum at 16+, although what is said could apply equally well to that at 18+. The recent proposals (Schools Council Working Paper No. 46) for a Certificate of Extended Education (C.E.E.) build upon the approach and methods used in C.S.E., and although disappointingly subject based they provide great possibilities for the extension of integrated courses into the sixth form. It would be easy to place the blame for this lack of integration in the sixth form solely upon the existing external examination system, but this would oversimplify the problem which cannot be considered without reference to the whole organizational structure of secondary education in Britain in the period under consideration, and to the uses that are made of the results of the examinations. The examination system is, nevertheless, an important factor and it was inevitable that questions would be asked about the external assessment of integrated courses as they developed.

For the teacher working to introduce and assess new courses, whether integrated or not, in a nationally recognized examination the period from the mid-1950s to the mid-1960s was a depressing one. There was little or nothing to show for much hard work and a great deal of frustration was generated. From the mid-1960s the situation slowly improved, but this improvement was slowest in relation to integrated proposals since the difficulties which faced those working to innovate both within the classroom and within the examining system were most marked in this area. The key issues may be summed up briefly as follows:

1 Syllabuses
2 Methods of Assessment
3 Equivalence

For the purposes of description and discussion these have been artificially separated here. In reality, however, they interacted continually upon each other and at different times they assumed differing degrees of importance.

Syllabuses

The issues associated with syllabus development are of long standing. At the secondary level syllabuses have in the main been produced for examinations. In this form they are in essence a contract between examiner and candidate laying down the areas of content and more recently the skills which the examiner is entitled to explore and assess, but to which he is at the same time limited. Teachers in this situation act as go-betweens or mediums who transmit the examiner's intent to their pupils, taking advantage of their experience of the system to use the teaching strategies they think most suitable for the purpose. The teaching syllabus thus emerges from a study of the examination syllabus and does not determine it. In consequence the systematic preparation of teaching syllabuses has been neglected by the profession, with adverse effects upon curriculum and course development and upon evaluation. Examining boards have attempted in recent years to reduce the influence of the examination syllabus, either by providing little in the way of information or by endeavouring to make it approximate more nearly to a teaching syllabus. We have, for example, examination syllabuses of such resounding lack of detail as 'British History 1867–1964. The major emphasis will be upon domestic political events but some knowledge of economic and social topics and foreign affairs will also be expected.' We also have examination syllabuses covering several pages in which both content and skills are spelt out in meticulous detail together with examples of how each topic might be treated. A good example of this second approach is provided by the Associated Examining Board's science syllabuses. Neither of these, however, solves the fundamental problem of how to match assessment to the aims of the curriculum and the courses which emerge from it, but instead they merely reflect our preference for writing examination rather than teaching syllabuses. The potential dangers of both approaches are obvious. In the first case question papers, as the only evidence available of an explicit view of what the two lines in the syllabus imply, are likely to assume an undue importance. In the second case, the very clarity and detail of the route marked out is an open encouragement for the teacher to follow it slavishly. It is much easier, moreover, to succumb to temptations such as these if the group being taught is of borderline potential in relation to the examination being taken. This is of less significance in an examination such as C.S.E. which does not embody a pass–fail standard, but even here the emphasis placed upon levels of performance as reflected in the award of grades is often excessive.

What these approaches to syllabuses provision neglect is any consideration of the purpose of teaching a particular subject at a particular stage. The undesirable results of this neglect can well be illustrated by the case of foreign languages. In general as a nation our command of languages is inadequate. This is partly due to our failure to decide why German, say, should be learnt by pupils between the ages of eleven and eighteen. Is it so that they can read German literature? Is it so that they can visit Germany and be able to enjoy conversation with German people? Is it to learn something of the German people through a study in their own language of German history, geography, political organization and culture? Or is it perhaps a survival of the view that a study of grammar and syntax of both ancient and modern languages provides the right fare for growing children at any particular level? It is only when we start to ask and answer questions such as these that we can begin to take a synoptic view of the curriculum as an essential first step to planning and taking decisions upon teaching strategies, course outcomes and methods of assessment.

Two further problems arise from examination syllabuses. First, they rarely give much indication of the balance between breadth and depth to be adopted in the study of the subject concerned. Again the examination paper can be turned to for aid, but it is only helpful in part since the mark scheme applied to the paper by the examiner is very rarely available. Secondly, an examination syllabus by its very nature tends to be confined to what is examinable. This, in combination with the limited range of assessment techniques in use until recently, has placed severe restrictions upon what is assessed, and thus in practice upon what is taught.

Enough has been said to show that these problems exist in respect of syllabuses for subjects for which there is a recognized body of content and upon the teaching of which there is a substantial fund of experience. It takes little thought to appreciate that such difficulties are likely to increase when related to syllabuses for newly introduced and hence often ill-defined integrated courses. For them the development of any widely applicable, content based syllabus is virtually impossible; indeed it is doubtful whether any external agency should attempt to prescribe one. The first task therefore for any teacher or group of teachers wishing to introduce a course in, say, social studies, whether it is to be assessed or not, is clearly the preparation of an appropriate teaching syllabus which should contain a statement of the ground which the course is intended to cover. A statement of content, however, is of itself insufficient. Any worthwhile teaching syllabus must also consider course objectives, course outcomes, teaching materials and teaching strategies. Moreover, to ask and provide answers to a question such as 'What is it that pupils who have been exposed to a particular course of study can do after it that they could not do before it?' is not of much worth unless an attempt is also made to find out whether the aims of the course have been achieved in practice and, if so, to what extent. This requires a review of objectives, outcomes, methods and material, and must involve in some form or other assessment for evaluative purposes. This leads us to the second issue.

Methods of Assessment

Whether assessment involves an external examination or not must be a matter for teachers and their schools to decide. Prior to 1965, however, the option to assess teacher-developed courses did not really exist, since C.S.E. Mode 3 did not exist. It is true that the regulations of the G.C.E. boards made provision at 'O' level for special syllabuses, or Mode 2 to use the current jargon. These were not, however, designed to promote innovation either in subject matter or in the assessment technique used. Instead they provided the opportunity to introduce minor variations within traditional subject areas, for example a local history option in history, or a different list of set books in English. But there were a few straws in the wind. In 1965 the Joint Matriculation Board started work on its new experimental 'O' level English syllabus. By 1973 this had eliminated a formal examination for several thousand candidates. In 1967 the Associated Examining Board introduced sociology at the Advanced Level. These were, however, experiments and their impact for several years was minimal.

Without the stimulus provided by nationally recognized certification it was all too easy for those developing courses to neglect the assessment aspects and evaluation. This did not, of course, apply universally and, as was mentioned in Chapter 2, the growth of local examinations in the later 1950s and early 1960s provided opportunities for collaborative effort. However, only a minority, for whom the opportunity to participate directly in the assessment of their own pupils did occur were affected. For most teachers there was nothing between the external examination and their own resources, the latter being very limited in terms of assessment. Moreover the more innovative the course the more difficult the assessment.

This was particularly the case when several subjects or disciplines were involved. Here curricula and the courses generated by them tended to place less emphasis upon factual knowledge and the ability to display it logically and accurately. Instead they were concerned with concepts, processes and skills emphasizing such things as enquiry. Speaking and doing almost always played a larger part than asking and listening. The implications of such differences for assessment are far reaching both in respect of the nature and extent of the techniques to be used and of the role to be played by the teacher.

During this period of the '50s and '60s very few teachers had experience which equipped them to tackle problems of assessment effectively, and the existing training agencies were in no position to fill the gaps. This situation undoubtedly adversely affected the potential for effective innovation in C.S.E., and is only now being slowly remedied. It was not surprising therefore that although teachers became frustrated with the existing system no real impetus towards introducing new homespun curricula within schools developed. Interesting proposals were too often stunted by being confined to only a part of the ability range, by being abandoned after the first two years of secondary education, by lack of help for those concerned with their introduction or by a combination of these factors.

Equivalence

The third issue, that of equivalence, created further difficulties. For L. A. Smith these were highlighted in the mid-1950s in discussions with the College of Preceptors on their proposals for a possible new Certificate of Education. The problem was that of evaluating and quantifying the equivalence of an integrated programme of study in terms of existing subjects. Moreover where external examinations were concerned the content of the existing subjects tended to be what was published in the syllabuses of the examining board concerned. In the case of G.C.E. further restrictions resulted from the maintenance of a list of approved subjects together with a set of criteria which had to be applied to any new subject proposed for G.C.E. examination. In these circumstances additional approval for both syllabus and subject had to be obtained from the Secondary Schools Examinations Council and later the Schools Council. When C.S.E. was introduced this control did not apply to it. A decision was taken in 1971 after discussion with the G.C.E. boards to remove it at 'O' level, although at 'A' level Schools Council approval for both syllabus and subject must still be obtained at the time of writing.

Educationally the attempt to achieve equivalence is a futile exercise, but in a world which counts and makes use of numbers of subjects and levels of pass it has a real significance. It became clear to L. A. S. (as it would have done to anyone else dealing with an examining board at that time) that their existing mechanism for considering new proposals was organized on a subject basis. It becomes clear also that these 'subject panels' wished to have their pound of disciplinary flesh, and were not disposed to grant their seal of approval unless they could apply criteria similar to those which they used for their existing syllabuses. In such circumstances the only way for any integrated course to be certified if it met with approval (and this was a substantial if) was for it to be described under some 'umbrella' title which would appear as a single line on the certificate. Thus, as far as the certificate was concerned, and in consequence more often than not as far as the user of the certificate was concerned, it became a single subject, regardless of the amount of time that had been devoted to it in school. The disadvantages of this require no further underlining.

The reader of this chapter will not now be surprised to learn that those teachers who tried to assess courses of their own devising at the secondary level through nationally recognized external examinations achieved virtually nothing in practical terms in the ten years or so prior to 1965. Work done during this period, however, disheartening it may have been for those concerned, served to identify a number of issues whose implementation or solution seemed essential if future attempts were to meet with more success. These were as follows:

1 The need for co-operation. New courses are unlikely to be developed or assessed by individuals working in isolation; ideas, experiences, materials, teaching strategies all must be shared. In this way they are subjected to the constructive criticism of colleagues which alone can lead to lasting improvement.
2 The need for help, advice and above all training for teachers in curriculum development, course construction and assessment procedures and techniques.
3 The need to reconsider the role of the teacher as assessor and the relationship that should exist between teachers and examining boards.
4 The inadequacy of global judgements upon the capabilities of individuals.
5 The need to hasten slowly. Innovation in education will only make itself felt if it can be diffused among a wide cross-section of the teaching profession. This is inevitably a slow process.

For these issues to become more than merely academic talking points, a changed environment was needed. This was to be provided by the introduction of C.S.E. Their full significance has, however, yet to be appreciated. Indeed, at the time of writing probably the most crucial issue of all, 'the role of the teacher as assessor' has not been debated seriously by the teaching profession as a whole, and 1974, we should remind ourselves, is ten years after C.S.E., 'the teacher controlled' examination, was first taken by pupils.

Meanwhile what was the other author doing? In common with the other G.C.E. Examining Boards the Associated Examining Board was beginning, as we saw in Chapter 2, to investigate new assessment techniques, particularly that of objective testing. After 1965 it also began to receive requests from schools to assess new courses developed by them in new ways. The origins of the A.E.B., which was founded in part to meet the same needs that C.S.E. was designed to meet, but which inevitably in the early 1950s were expressed in a less developed form, made it inherently more sympathetic to new ideas than the then more traditional university-based boards. It was also fortunate in having a secretary who believed that his staff should constantly concern themselves with the educational implications of what they were doing. In consequence the opportunities for experimental work increased rapidly.

Such work drew attention to very much the same issues that had arisen from the teachers' experiences. The need for co-operation, for training, for the greater involvement of teachers in the assessment process, for the use of a wider range of techniques, was as great for examining boards as it was for teachers. Initially, however, the training programmes put forward by examining boards had only one end in view, to improve the quality of the examinations which they provided. Teachers might receive useful professional training in addition, but this was a by-product. This notion and the existing view of the role of an examining board were both questionable; for H. G. M. this became apparent when the first Mode 3s were submitted to the A.E.B. To the G.C.E. boards Mode 3s (if they were willing to accept them) presented a means whereby experimental work, which would have been extremely difficult and expensive to undertake on a large scale, could be undertaken on a small scale under carefully controlled conditions. Any information gained and lessons learned could then be fed back into the main stream of the board's work. To the schools on the other hand Mode 3 represented freedom, and it was impossible for anyone concerned with Mode 3 development, as H. G. M. was at the A.E.B. between 1966 and 1970, to be other than impressed both by the potential revealed and by the difficulties involved.

All G.C.E. boards during the period 1966–70 were obtaining assistance where they could find it, in some cases from the United States. They all had, however, one, or sometimes more than one, particular subject areas, in which they conducted experimental work from the outset on their own, as a means of identifying the problems involved in such activities as defining objectives, test construction, item analysis and planning training courses. This experience then provided the basis for a programme for the board's work in other subject areas. In the case of the A.E.B. the particular subject was history, and between 1967–71 the board had an ongoing programme of developmental work in history with particular reference to skills testing and the use of documentary evidence in assessment. This led to the introduction in 1972 of an alternative syllabus at 'O' level in economic and social history. It also led to the establishment of a project on the assessment of world history at 'O' level, which was to provide the two authors, as the next two chapters will show, with a crucial link in the chain between the potential of exploiting the existing examination system and the reality of doing so in practice.

Before this project got under way, however, the two authors had made their first contact over the possibility of assessing inter-disciplinary enquiry (I.D.E.). Discussion of this problem caused them to start to systematize their thinking and to try to develop some rationale for course development through the agency of the external examination system. L. A. S. after helping in the first four pilot courses on curriculum development held under D.E.S. auspices at Goldsmiths' College, became in 1966 one of the founders of the Curriculum Laboratory there and one of the creators of the Fourfold Curriculum of which, as we have seen, enquiry was the central pillar. From the outset he was involved in problems of assessment. It soon became clear to the staff of the Laboratory that unless means of assessing I.D.E. were devised, its development would be slow and many secondary schools would not continue it beyond their third year. I.D.E., as we have already seen, was sharply contrasted both with any attempt to diminish the importance of the disciplines as coherent intellectual or aesthetic systems, and with a merely integrated curriculum which denied to students the discovery of relationships and the satisfaction of collaborative exploration. Group, as well as individual enquiry, was its essence, causing a class lesson to become the exception and students to spend most of their time working in small groups. Such a pattern posed severe problems for assessment.

Under pressure L. A. S. became in effect the spokesman for the schools who wished to assess I.D.E. in public examinations. In C.S.E. this was obviously possible under Mode 3 arrangements, although progress was slow, largely because the organizational pattern of C.S.E. boards, as with G.C.E. was designed to deal with subject-based proposals rather than those which involved several disciplines. The extreme flexibility, moreover, of the I.D.E. programme made it impossible to prespecify all the outcomes, a process normally regarded as essential in any Mode 3 submission. In G.C.E. assessment was also theroretically possible with those boards which accepted Mode 3. L. A .S. therefore decided to approach the A.E.B. This led to an exchange of papers, correspondence and visits upon which the authors' subsequent collaboration was founded.[1] In making this approach L. A. S. had to forget the need to hasten slowly, and took as his starting point for a collaborative venture in assessment probably the most difficult exercise he could have devised. This action, as the next chapter describes, was to lead initially to failure and in consequence to an apparent dead end. The way ahead was to be shown by a number of rather less ambitious schemes in particular that put forward by the Hedley Walter School.

[1] The two principal documents involved 'A proposal for externally examining I.D.E. and integrated studies' and 'inter-disciplinary enquiry' are produced as Appendix 1. Although they emerged from correspondence between the two authors and formed a part of it, the two documents were not written in response to each other. They have a very dated look about them today, but at the time they pin-pointed a number of crucial problems that faced the development of examinations for integrated studies.

CHAPTER FOUR

Turning Point

The practical application of inter-disciplinary enquiry (I.D.E.) in 1968 was restricted to a number of experiments in schools scattered throughout the country, but it was already evident that a two year I.D.E. programme for the 14–16 year old age group in secondary schools could not be spelled out in the detail required by examining boards at that time. The fact that I.D.E. was seen as being an open-ended approach to education, with a potential for providing an alternative to teacher-structured lessons, found it a place in many schools. There was ample evidence to suggest that the development of I.D.E., and the Fourfold Curriculum of which it was a part, created exciting conditions for innovative work. Such work not only enabled hitherto neglected areas to be tackled, but also provided an opportunity for teachers and students jointly to make their work in familiar areas more lively, ambitious and imaginative. A rich diet thus awaited the teacher who knew how to develop the approach that I.D.E. embodied. It could not, however, be examined, at least not in the terms of its own objectives, as the correspondence between the two authors revealed. The time was not ripe for the kind of experimentation which alone could produce a viable scheme of assessment satisfactory to board and school alike. I.D.E. proposals were by the very nature unable to meet the existing requirements of almost all examining boards both G.C.E. and C.S.E., namely that:

1 The schemes of work and proposals for assessment had to be submitted for consideration months if not years ahead of the time when the students concerned would take their terminal assessment.
2 The schemes of work had to be set out so that they could be subjected to analysis either by subject panels or individual subject specialists both as to content and standards in terms of the board's existing syllabuses.
3 The methods of assessment proposed had to be clearly stated and examples provided at the time when the scheme of work was originally submitted.

In 1968, even with a concentrated effort on the massive theme 'Living in a Technological Society'[1] it was only possible to offer an examining board a 'declaration of intent' on the way the studies within any given school would unfold during a two year period. Moreover, it was only by actually working the course with the students that the teachers concerned could find the means to start the process of assessing performance. The problem was further compounded by the use of group work within I.D.E. programmes. This often made it difficult for teachers to pin-point the contribution of a particular individual, an essential requirement for assessment involving individual certification. Again, only time spent working on these problems could lay the foundations upon which to develop adequate solutions.

The response of the Associated Examining Board to the proposals put forward by L. A. S., as a study of the documents in Appendix 1 will show, made progress with I.D.E. impossible. While bitterly disappointing, particularly as the scheme was designed to provide the conditions under which a programme of developmental work could have been undertaken, this reaction was understandable. Indeed, looking back it is difficult to see how those concerned could have come to any other decision. The work undertaken in the Curriculum Laboratory on 'Living in a Technological Society' had, it is true, shown that it was possible to forecast some 60 per cent or 70 per cent of the main-stream studies that a two year course on the theme could promote. It had, however, also underlined the infinite variety of approaches that could be undertaken by schools and had done nothing to suggest that any useful basis could be worked out for comparison between course coverage of the theme and existing G.C.E. subjects. Neither could those involved state with any clarity ways in which the studies promoted by this I.D.E. exercise could be assessed in terms of student performance. Nevertheless, despite the uncertainties occasioned by new methods and new materials and the frustrations caused by a failure to devise a viable programme for assessment, considerable enthusiasm was generated by those who were trying to realize the potential which they believed existed in I.D.E. The authors were thus encouraged to continue to worry away at the problem of assessment. This meant returning to first base.

First base in this context meant going back to subject-based examinations. In making this apparently retrograde step the authors were greatly influenced by the emergence of a spirited and ultimately successful attempt by the headmaster and staff of the Hedley Walter Comprehensive School in Brentwood, Essex, to have a school-devised integrated studies programme examined under Mode 3 arrangements by both the Associated Examining Board and the East Anglian C.S.E. Board. This programme so

[1] *Ideas* Nos. 11 and 12 (combined), Goldsmiths' College, Feb., 1969.

ably steered by Arthur Gregson, the headmaster, through the various channels of the 'examination establishment' was seen by the authors as a viable starting point from which to set out again.

The Hedley Walter programme as put to the A.E.B. and as subsequently developed in the school[1] does not claim to be, and certainly is not I.D.E. It asked for certification in four subjects: English language, history, geography and religious education. A scheme of work covering the fourth and fifth years details the progression of each of these subjects, so that at times their material content is presented as if it were fused together. In broad terms, therefore, it was possible for the school to put on paper a complex programme of integrated studies which could be itemized under four subject headings. This whole programme constituted the offer made to the examining boards for external certification under Mode 3 arrangements in four subjects, all of which were recognizable and acceptable. This meant that the school could argue its case for certification of work done on a subject basis without reference except in very general terms to the approaches it proposed to adopt in presenting the material content of the scheme to its pupils. This approach of course differed markedly from the approaches adopted hitherto for the assessment of I.D.E., where the declaration of intent was open-ended and syllabuses did not exist. The acceptance of the scheme in 1968 by both boards with the blessing of the Schools Council as far as the G.C.E. side was concerned was a significant event. For the first time the external examining system was used to assess a school-based integrated curriculum. Freedom and external certification were thus compatible. It would not be unfair to call the strategy adopted a negative one. The reason for this is not that its requirements were undemanding for either examining boards or school, but that it had limitations as will be shown later. These limitations stemmed in the main from the fact that it operated within the existing subject-orientated system. Yet ironically this was also its greatest strength because it gave the impression that the system was secure whilst embarking on work that contained great potential for change. The main feature of the strategy was that it centred round the use of existing subjects as connoted by the syllabuses of the various examining boards. These were accepted by all and sundry as being descriptive of the subjects if not the disciplines to which they referred. Of course, the validity of the claim of any syllabus to speak for the subject whose name it bears is debatable, but is not the issue here. What is important is that it is the basis upon which examining boards create syllabuses, compile examinations and award certificates!

Making use of the accepted practices of agencies or individuals who are in a position to take decisions is, of course, a well-established strategem

[1] *Dialogue*, No. 10 (Schools Council), Spring 1972.

for those who wish to bring about changes in an evolutionary fashion. Such an approach is not without its dangers, particularly in relation to the degree of compromise required of those who adopt it. It has, however, the redeeming feature that using it produces a greater understanding of the situation within which it operates which makes progress likely to be faster and more profitable with each succeeding attempt. The strategy used by Hedley Walter thus made it easier both for themselves and for other schools to inch their way towards an understanding and realization of what for them constituted a freer curriculum. The fact that surprisingly few schools took advantage of this opportunity, particularly in respect of G.C.E., does not detract from its significance.

This negative strategy, therefore, for all its limitations, must be seen as an essential preliminary to a positive strategy or strategies. This applies especially in an educational system such as that which exists in England and Wales, where the development of positive initiatives by established institutions is viewed with suspicion if not hostility. One has only to look at the role of the inspectorate to underline this point. In curriculum development terms, therefore, each school sees its potential differently and must develop innovation from the standpoint of its existing practice. Such a situation can create obstacles to change as well as potential for change. If positive strategies are to emerge in any area of educational development, the agencies involved must appreciate and respect the features of a school's existing way of life and seek to use them as the prime agency for change. This is no easy task since the dividing line between advice and direction is paper thin, and nowhere is this more apparent than in the relations that exist between examining boards and the schools which use them. Every ounce of potential must, therefore, be squeezed out of any successful strategy, however negative it may be, before one can adopt a more positive posture. This is what the rest of this chapter will try to do at the risk of being slightly repetitive. In this way the agencies involved, here schools and examining boards, can re-think their respective roles in an evolutionary rather than a revolutionary environment.

Negative strategies do not, however, involve doing nothing. In the situation we are considering practical ways must be found of creating a meeting ground between teachers in schools and those who work on the development and organization of external examinations. Indeed, in the long term this meeting ground must be between those who work in schools and those who work in the education service outside schools. Only thus can a two-way traffic of ideas develop. Such a traffic means that none of the institutions concerned can afford to be passive. Teachers wishing to assess their own courses must first perceive and then articulate both the existing conditions within their schools and the objectives towards which they wish to strive through their curriculum. Gathering such information and putting it into communicable form are not easy exercises, but they are the essential preliminaries to the start of a dialogue. (Dialogue is a much over-used word in education today; all too often it is a synonym for monologue. In this context, however, there is no real alternative to its use in describing what must be a genuine educational debate between two groups of people.) The examining boards too have a role to play additional to that which they have played historically. They must press teachers to articulate their requirements to the point where no misunderstanding is left on either side. This may well turn out to be a slow and on occasion a painful process, since it is one with which most teachers are unfamiliar and which not all may welcome. When it has been done the board can suggest methods of assessment thought to be suitable for the school's needs. Then under Mode 3 arrangements, it is the school's responsibility to develop the methods which it finally chooses to use. The boards' role here can vary greatly in its impact, according to the quality of its advice and the range of the services which it can provide. The skills and environment needed for educational consultancy of this kind are foreign to examining boards, indeed many of them have yet to accept that this is something they should do. No well-tried recipes for success in this situation as yet exist. This may be no disadvantage, however, if both school and board are prepared to grope mutually for solutions which often trial and error will make successful. The learning that can result from this process is immense and will be reflected in improved teaching methods and assessment practices.

One of the most significant contributions that a school can make to the dialogue is in the organization and comprehensiveness of its original submission. If this is well thought through and clearly set out, discussion will start on the right footing. If not, misunderstanding can easily arise. The original submission inevitably involves a school in extensive prior internal discussion, but it is time well spent. This is particularly necessary with an integrated programme which requires teachers of different subjects to interact in different ways. Of course, there can be no standard form of layout for such submissions. Each scheme, like the school or schools from which it comes, is different. There are, however, certain features which ought to find a place within any proposal made by a school to a board and these are considered in the paragraphs which follow in the context of an integrated programme.

First, there should be a detailed description of the integrated programme designed to reveal the way the teachers themselves perceive the way the subject matter they have chosen is inter-related. With this information there should also be presented some indication of the approaches that will be employed when the programme is made operational, say over a two year period. However, this does not require any detail of the sequence in which the material is to be presented. In essence, a scheme of work is wanted, rather than a syllabus. Only through such a submission can those looking at it start to gain an insight into the intentions of the teachers who have created the programme. It will not have escaped notice that so far no statement such as 'aims and objectives should be stated with the utmost clarity' has been made. The authors recognize that the process of stating aims and objectives is a terribly difficult one to accomplish in relation to an integrated programme. It seems much more realistic to assume that only the broad aims of such a programme together with a few more specific objectives can and indeed should be formulated by the teachers in the initial submission. Other objectives will emerge in discussion between board and teachers, and others still will not be clearly articulated until the programme itself is under way.

Secondly, there should be a breakdown of the programme in terms of the various, separate subjects that it claims to involve. This breakdown should be presented under subject headings and in terms which are used in published Mode 1 syllabuses. In doing this teachers will find that their programme embraces the subjects concerned in irregular patterns; some subjects will be haevily represented within the overall programme, others will be present only as traces. In addition it is quite likely that teachers will find within their programme certain aspects, especially in the field of inter-relationships, which defy categorization under existing subject headings.

As a result of its breakdown of the programme into subject terms the school will be in a position to submit proposals for subject certification to the examining board, and to continue its discussions a stage further. In C.S.E. the actual description that is permissible on the certificate is much more widely ranging that in G.C.E. where the single subject remains the norm. This makes it possible for schools, if they wish to do so, to describe relatively exactly on their C.S.E. certificates the nature of their courses. They still must, however, take account of the effect of such descriptions upon the user. Most schools in consequence prefer to use subject titles. By so doing they are required to spell out their courses in subject terms in the way suggested in the last paragraph.

This exercise calls attention to the problem of what the authors have called 'overs and unders'. It will soon become apparent to the teachers that one or more of the subject syllabuses which have emerged is going to ask more from the students than would its equivalent Mode 1. Such a subject is English language. The article in *Dialogue* No. 10 which describes the Hedley Walter programme shows that their pupils did more work in English language than they would have been asked to do in G.C.E. or

C.S.E. in this subject. English language was, therefore, over-subscribing in terms of its demands. No formula has yet been devised to give the student credit for the extra work involved save by the award of higher grades. More serious is the problem of under-subscription. This results when an evaluation of the scheme reveals that one or more of the subjects claimed for certification falls short of the demands made by the equivalent Mode 1. This situation can only be met by offering within the programme opportunities for students to undertake further studies in the under-subscribed subjects if they wish to obtain certification in them. The danger of this is that a distortion will be introduced into the programme in the interests of certification. In the case of the Hedley Walter programme religious education was the under-subscribed subject, and more time had to be directed to the formal assessment of this subject than it might necessarily have warranted in relation to its weight in the course as a whole. Only the school can decide how far such a distortion can be taken and only a board can decide what it considers should be the minimum requirements for certification in any one subject. This issue is therefore likely to form a crucial aspect of the dialogue. Any response made by an examining board to a school in 'the dialogue' must be continuous and open. Open means that the school knows the processes and the people involved, and has the opportunity at all times to question those who are giving advice on behalf of the board. Those who give this advice ought normally to help subsequently with the moderation of the results of the course in terms of pupil performance, after the scheme has been approved. If this is done, a successful accommodation all along the line from initial approval to the final award of grades will result from an educational debate, rather than from the application of mechanical or administrative criteria.

This describes the Hedler Walter strategy used to its maximum advantage. It forms a sufficient basis upon which to run a successful integrated programme and have the results certificated by both C.S.E. and G.C.E. boards. It has, however, limitations. What in essence has happened as a result of the exercise just described is that a school has carried out a comparative analysis of its own programme and the syllabuses of an examining board or boards. It has almost certainly been able to do this along only the one dimension of content, for this is how most examining boards' syllabuses are presented. In recent years it is true that there has been a slow but steady increase in the number of syllabuses which also list the skills which the boards propose to test, but these still remain a minority. Where this is done a more widely ranging comparison can be made, and more attention can be devoted to exploring the depth of understanding required by the course. This last point can also be explored through a comparison of the past papers of the examining boards and the assessment proposals of the school. Nevertheless, this is likely to be a very limited exercise because of differences between the objectives of the school programme and the boards' syllabuses, which affect the techniques of assessment used. Many integrated programmes, moreover, are as concerned with concepts and relationships as they are with skills and information. Differences enough occur when content and skills are compared. How much greater and more significant are the differences when we start to look at the concepts teachers think to be important, and the way they interrelate different subject areas in their courses! In such circumstances a strategy which can do little more than compare content and skills and which is over-concerned with subject descriptions is unlikely to produce the kind of understanding required. Something more positive is needed from the school submission and from the examining board's response. The outlines of such a positive strategy seemed to the authors to emerge from the A.E.B. World History Project. This will be considered in the next chapter.

CHAPTER FIVE

A Pilot Study in World History

The origins of the A.E.B. World History Project were not out of the ordinary. It is true that as it operates in 1973 the project has certain unusual features; for example, the nature and extent of teacher involvement in what is a Mode 1, the function of the syllabus and the assessment pattern adopted. These can, however, be found in other projects and are in no sense unique. More significant are certain ideas that emerged from the discussions of the working party responsible for the project. These seemed to offer the possibility of collaborative curriculum development between examining boards and schools, more positive and more stimulating than that implicit in the Hedley Walter 'model'. That in the end this vision appealed to no more than the two authors meant that the project did not carry the possibility into practice. The reasons for this are in themselves of importance since they underline the efforts required for a positive strategy and the dangers that can result if one of the two partners becomes too dominant.

The project originated with a working party set up by the A.E.B. in the summer of 1968 to investigate methods of assessment in history with particular reference to the 13–16 year old age group. It had a membership of eleven, four of whom were then currently teaching history in secondary schools, one of whom was teaching history in a further education establishment and four of whom were lecturing in history at colleges of education (all these last had had recent teaching experience in secondary schools). The remaining two members were the authors. L. A. S. was then at Goldsmiths' with the Curriculum Laboratory and H. G. M. with the A.E.B.: the latter acted as secretary to the working party until the end of 1970. Six of the members had been engaged or were engaged in investigations into problems of assessment in history either on their own or as part of a specific programme. Their experience of current examining practices was wide, including the development of Mode 3s in history in G.C.E. and C.S.E. as well as work at the assistant and chief examiner level in both examinations.

In terms of the teaching of history the working party contained both those who believed that history was a unique discipline which ought not to be tampered with and those who regarded it as supplying a distinctive perspective, basically comparative, to an integrated programme. Among the latter there were also differences between those who regarded an integrated programme as an amalgam of subjects in which at particular times different subjects played the leading role, and those who regarded it as essentially a vehicle for enquiry-based learning with the content being comparatively unimportant. Courses of the latter type (it had been suggested earlier in the book) are better called inter-disciplinary rather than integrated.

The brief given to the working party by the A.E.B. was an open-ended one with no specific requirement to provide proposals for assessment. Initially therefore the discussions were concerned with broad general issues such as 'Why do we teach history in schools for the 13–16 year old age range?' and 'What might pupils be able to do at the end of, say, a two year course in history which they could not do at its beginning?' This led eventually to the formulation by the working party of five fairly general aims which it was considered could usefully form a basis for more specific statements of objectives. These latter objectives might be put forward by teachers working to construct and subsequently evaluate courses in history of their own choosing, or by an examining board as its statement of intent for the assessment of a syllabus.

The five aims were as follows:

1 to foster an understanding of the significance of change and continuity for historical study;
2 to promote an awareness of the availability of primary and secondary sources;
3 to encourage the use and evaluation of materials of various types;
4 to elicit from the student imaginative and emphathetic responses;
5 to encourage students to communicate their personal understanding and involvement through historical study.

The early meetings of the working party underlined once again how difficult many teachers find the definition of aims and objectives. They also highlighted the problem of deciding how specific or how generalized statements of objectives ought to be, particularly when put forward by an examining board as information for schools. While stimulating and interesting, however, these discussions were in danger of ending in a vacuum because they were theoretical rather than practical in scope. It was now necessary to look at the realization of the proposed aims in terms of providing an actual examination upon a selected area of history. To this end the working party decided to concentrate on twentieth century World history taking as their title 'The History of World Powers and World Events in the Twentieth Century'. They also decided to recommend to the A.E.B. that the board should sponsor a pilot 'O' level examination on this topic, involving initially about twenty-five schools and colleges of further education. This recommendation was accepted, and from it stemmed the project proper. There were two main reasons for the choice of twentieth century world history. First, courses in world history were making an increasing appeal to schools and colleges of further education for both the 13–16 and the 16–19 year old age range. This was partly due to the search for so-called 'relevance' in the curriculum, but partly also to the enormous range of courses which could be developed under the umbrella of world history and the scope for inter-disciplinary work that could result. Secondly, courses in world history posed severe assessment problems, particularly if the flexibility that was one of their major attractions was to be preserved. It was thus a topic peculiarly suited to co-operative activity between school and examining board.

After the meeting immediately following the decision to concentrate upon twentieth century world history the members of the working party produced proposals for the assessment of the 'five aims'. These proposals suggested that, provided the aims were spelt out in more specific terms, they could be assessed largely through written questions although of a kind rather different from those used in the current 'O' level examination. It also seemed desirable to most members that a place should be found for project work or individual study and the criteria used for assessment of these would need to be carefully considered. It now began to dawn on the working party that the core of the problem remained unsolved and indeed largely untouched. If an examining board were to produce and assess a syllabus on something as wide-ranging as twentieth century world powers and problems, it could scarcely do so on the basis of a statement of content which was hitherto the traditional way of presenting an examination syllabus. Such a statement would have to be either so general as to be largely meaningless, or so prescriptive as to impose restrictions which would almost certainly be unacceptable to many. Allied to the syllabus was its assessment. How did one set about producing 'an examination', whatever its component parts, which matched up to the almost endless choice of topics open to schools, if one had no syllabus upon which to base it? There were several possible approaches, the most obvious of which was a Mode 3 for each school. This had to be excluded here since it would not have provided a model for a co-operative examining board/school exercise other than on a one to one basis. Another possibility was to use questions which either provided the candidates with the content upon which their answers were to be based or allowed them to use a variety of illustrations. An example of the latter type of question would be one upon 'revolutions' rather than one upon 'the Russian Revolution' or 'the Chinese Revolution'. This would enable a candidate to use his own 'revolutionary' illustration or illustrations. Even so the range of questions would have to be extensive, and they would inevitably be uneven in the demand that they made upon the candidates. The individual study or project would also provide candidates with opportunities to pursue topics of their own choosing as would the use of course work as part of the assessment. Assessment techniques could thus be found to cope with the problem, but this would have been to put the cart before the horse. The question that mattered was what was being assessed. Two possible bases for marrying flexibility with common assessment would be to formulate a syllabus either in terms of skills or in terms of concepts, and then to test either the acquisition of these skills or the understanding of those concepts. These two possibilities are here treated as if they were separate but in practice they could be combined. If the syllabus and the assessment were to be based upon defined skills, then the five general aims would have to be translated into a specific set of behavioural objectives. If a concept approach was to be used, then the first stage would have to be the indentification of key concepts and the second (as with the skills) the devising of appropriate assessment.

Neither of these two suggestions is easy to accomplish in practice. A look at the five general aims, for example, will show that certain of them, notably 3, and to a lesser extent 4, can readily be re-defined in terms of the skills necessary to achieve the aim in question. There would, moreover, be a large measure of agreement among teachers as to what the appropriate skills were. Others, notably 1, are less susceptible to this kind of pragmatic definition, although this should not be an excuse for giving up. The danger, however, of trying, and more particularly of succeeding, is that the ensuing statement of skills (or concepts for that matter) might be seen by many as constituting a more restrictive framework within which to teach a course than any statement of content even in an area as vast as world history.

L. A. S. 's experiences, described in Chapter 3, had suggested that the development of frameworks which could form a suitable basis for course and assessment construction, particularly where the emphasis was upon the acquisition of skills and concepts, was an area in which teachers wanted considerable help. A possible aid here where skills were concerned was the use of taxonomies. The term taxonomy is taken from the biological sciences, and means an orderly hierarchical classification. The taxonomies as developed by Bloom and his associates attempted to provide such a hierarchical classification in respect of educational objectives initially in the cognitive and later in the affective domain.[1] Others have followed this

---

[1] *Handbook I The Cognitive Domain* was published in Britain for the first time in 1956 although it was not until some twelve years later that it became familiar in British educational circles.
Handbook II The Affective Domain was first published in Britain in 1964.

example although none has become as well known. Educational taxonomies in general, and Bloom's work in particular, have attracted extremes of acceptance and rejection, neither of which has been particularly helpful in the search for models upon which to base the planning of courses and their evaluation. These extremes stem largely from the belief (which incidentally Bloom and his colleagues would have repudiated) that it is necessary to swallow any taxonomy whole and undigested. Taxonomies do not and were never intended to provide all the answers. Rather they are sources of ideas, encouraging the use of critical faculties and acting as a stimulus to thought about educational objectives. Their principal weakness is their artificiality, and Bloom's work in particular is almost certainly too detailed for everyday use. They can perhaps best be seen as pieces of starting equipment. Just as at the beginning of a journey to the moon a great deal of equipment is used and subsequently jettisoned, so taxonomies in their formal outlines should be thrown overboard after their principles have been grasped. If this does not happen then they will cease to be a stimulus and become instead a strait jacket.

In particular any attempt to use Bloom's or indeed any other unmodified taxonomy, as part of the model building process for integrated courses, is likely to retard progress. The first requirement in planning any course is to consider where it stands in the context of the total curriculum for the age range under consideration. This synoptic view, which is often neglected, is absolutely essential if overlap and wasteful duplication is to be avoided. Thereafter some trigger mechanism is required to generate ideas in a systematic fashion without creating a restrictive framework at the same time. In this process, which will permit the subsequent evaluation to be undertaken in relation to an organized pattern of objectives, taxonomies can play a part. Indeed, reflection upon the principles underlying taxonomies can generate ideas of considerable potential. They are not, however, the only possible trigger and other approaches will be suggested in the pages which follow.

Concepts arouse even more concern and hostility among teachers than do skills. An early approach adopted by L. A. S. in the late 1950s to try and allay these feelings was the development of conceptual maps. A conceptual map serves two basic purposes. First to suggest in conceptual terms the contributions that different disciplines might make to a suggested course, and second to draw attention to a variety of ways in which the course itself might be developed. The practical impact of these maps at the time when they were first tried out was small, since the subject specialists who taught the well entrenched subject disciplines in secondary schools were primarily concerned with content. Their use did, however, underline the inadequacies of existing approaches to assessment. So long as content remained king, then assessment techniques would remain restricted and public examinations could continue to be exclusively terminal and external. As soon as courses emphasize such things as concepts, process, enquiry and skills, then the need to extend the range of assessment techniques in use became essential and the value of the terminal test and the absence of teacher judgment in the determination of results came to be called in question.

To try to convince the world history working party that it was possible to devise syllabuses based upon the identification of key concepts and subsequently to assess whether these had been understood, L.A.S. produced what he called a 'matrix'. This is worth examining in some detail as a model for course construction, particularly where integration between disciplines is involved, since it provided the trigger mechanism referred to in the earlier discussion upon taxonomies. It thus represented a considerable refinement of the conceptual map.

As presented to the working party the matrix was designed to provide a basis for the development and assessment of a number of experimental G.C.E. 'O' level syllabuses using as their subject matter 'The History of World Powers and World Events in the Twentieth Century' and keeping in mind the five general aims. It was divided into five parts as follows:

1 Contained the stages for the development of a series of sets which reflected major concepts and areas of concern relevant to the subject matter under consideration.
2 Consisted of a statement of a possible scheme of work, presented in the form of a syllabus, for the subject 'World Powers and Events in the Twentieth Century'.
3 Presented a number of topics and patch studies which it was suggested might result from a consideration of the subject matter.
4 Gave examples of inter-disciplinary studies which could arise from Part A of the matrix.
5 Gave examples of special areas of study which could involve pupils in primary research.

It should be emphasized that the selection of the material involved in the matrix was essentially a personal matter for the author, and was only designed to provide illustrations of the methods of principles that the matrix suggested. For this reason only the outline of the matrix is set out here and not the material. The steps used to achieve the series of sets which formed the end product of Part A of the matrix were as follows:

(i) The setting down of a flow of ideas which were suggested by a consideration of the period concerned. The resulting list might well run into hundreds of headings which would normally consist of single words designed to indicate important concepts or areas of concern within the period, for example: nationalism, aggression, world war, distribution of wealth. Such a list would inevitably be uneven in terms of importance and there were bound to be substantial overlaps.

(ii) The grading of the ideas in the original list into sets or categories. The heading or the main idea within each particular set would be suggested by re-reading the list of ideas and by re-considering the period to be covered. The sets were thus in essence groups of related ideas or concepts. The different groups would, of course, still be interrelated in many ways but the process would lead to a considerable reduction in the number of headings.

(iii) The generating of possible examination questions by applying to the contents of the sets 'a generating model'. This model suggests that the understanding of concepts is best measured by reference to:

(a) institutions or organizations, in which a concept has been or is embodied;

(b) processes through which a concept is applied in any particular situation;

(c) situations in which a concept is being or has been applied;

(d) attitudes or values which have led to or originated from the application of a concept in a given situation.

In addition to suggesting possible questions, application of the generating model would also suggest further areas of concern which might in their turn lead to the enlarging of a particular set, and suggest still further questions. While many questions would be suggested by relating one of the points on its own to any one concept, many others would result from relating combinations of the points to combinations of concepts. Many of the questions would also involve a consideration of disciplines other than history and would require the use of analysis, the relationship of cause and effect and a comparative approach. Any questions suggested must also always keep in mind the objectives defined by the working party.

A practical illustration may serve to clarify the description given in the previous paragraph.

(a) Consideration of the list of ideas and the period might suggest that a key concept which ought to form the basis of a set is aggression. In the list are a number of words which could form part of this set for example, interference, fear, neutrality, balance of power These are grouped together.

(b) The generating model is then applied to aggression (and to the other parts of the set as required). This might suggest that an institution or organization in which aggression was implict was the Nazi Party; that a process through which aggression was applied was illustrated by reference to the Nazi treatment of the Jews over the period 1933–45; that a situation in which aggression was implicit was the seizure of power by Hitler in 1933; and that attitudes or values which might have led to aggression were embodied in the theories of the Master Race. These suggestions could themselves lead to much larger issues, such as what kinds of situation encourage or foster aggression, or what are the psychological or sociological basis of aggression. Practical expression of aggression in the form of wars is, moreover, frequent in the period under consideration.

In part B of the matrix, the suggested syllabus presented in sequence the following aspects of the period:

(a) The world powers in the twentieth century emerge
(b) Major confrontations between the world powers
(c) Economic developments of the twentieth century
(d) The growth of technological power
(e) The social and cultural consequences of world events and the development of standards of living in various parts of the world, with particular reference to the post-1929 period
(f) The emergent nations
(g) Tensions in the contemporary world

In Part C of the matrix, the suggested topics and patch studies were presented as forming together one approach to the study of history and to its possible assessment. The topics suggested were divided into two sections as follows:

(a) contained statements which invited candidates to take a linear or chronological approach in their answers;
(b) contained questions which posed problems which were likely to encourage candidates to enquire and use the various techniques of historical study.

Although in the matrix, the presentation of the suggested topics took the form of questions, the approach could be altered either to provide an alternative way of presenting the scheme of work, or to provide additional information for the pupils in helping them to understand the objectives of the course.

Part D of the matrix presented examples which were particularly suited to inter-disciplinary studies, but there was no reason why the whole of the material suggested in the matrix should not be treated in this way if required.

Part E required no further elaboration and was intended to provide illustrations of possible research studies which could be embodied in an assessment of candidates.

The proposals contained in the matrix could be objected to on the grounds that the key concepts themselves were not sufficiently well-defined, and that much of the suggested material was more appropriate to an inter-disciplinary than to a history course. They were indeed quite strongly criticised on both these counts by members of the working party. It was recognized, however, by even the most vehement critics that these were points of detail and of emphasis, and did not of themselves lessen the value of the matrix as an instrument for the production of experimental syllabuses and examinations. A much more important issue was whether individual teachers would feel able to use the matrix in the form in which it was presented to the working party. On balance the working party doubted this, and did not in the end recommend that it form a part of any proposals that might be made to schools. This, as will be seen later, was, in the opinion of the authors at least, a contributing factor in the failure of the project to realize its full potential as an agent for freeing the curriculum.

Before any school could be invited to take part in any experimental work, discussions on two important matters were still required; first, what should be the pattern of assessment, and second, exactly what information was the A.E.B. going to present to interested schools in lieu of a content syllabus. As far as the assessment structure was concerned, the matrix had reinforced the view expressed by the working party that the five general aims could be adequately assessed by means of written questions and a 'project', although it was necessary that the aims be spelled out in more specific terms for this purpose. What was not yet clear was whether this explication should be made primarily in terms of skills mastery or concept understanding, of neither or a mixture of both. Nor was it clear whether it should be made by the schools or by the A.E.B. After considerable discussion it was decided to confine the assessment at least initially to a written paper and a 'project', giving the written paper a weighting of 65 per cent and the 'project' a weighting of 35 per cent. It was further agreed that the written questions should range from ones in which candidates were asked to supply answers to questions to which there was not necessarily a correct answer, to others where they were asked to select from given information. The candidates' room for manœuvre in terms of the answers they were asked to provide would thus vary considerably.

The bulk of the discussion on assessment was not, however, devoted to the written paper, difficult as its construction would ultimately prove to be, but to the 'project'. Many of the working party, like many teachers, felt that the educational value of the 'project' had not been matched, in history at least, by equivalent success as a means of assessment. They had two reasons for this. The first stemmed from the view held by many educationists that a project should be unstructured if the maximum educational value for the child is to result. Such a viewpoint fails to appreciate that unstructured situations rarely come about by accident; if anything they require more careful planning than something which is apparently far less spontaneous. So it is with the project. Successful project work results not from the teachers leaving the child to get on with it but rather from careful selection of topics, from the provision of adequate and varied resource material and above all from teachers themselves acting as resources.

The second reason for doubting the value of the 'project' as a means of assessment was based on the emphasis that tends to be placed upon the finished product in the reward given to project work. This means that more work is often put into the descriptive and decorative aspects of, say, a history project than in to its planning, or into the search for relevant material and into the use that is made of the material. In a phrase, the end-product has become more important than the processes by which it was achieved. The working party was, therefore, concerned in its proposals for the assessment of the 'project' to emphasize the plan of campaign and the use of resources as well as the execution. A plan of campaign was moreover, not only to be supplied for the major 'project' which each candidate would complete but also for at least two other studies which would remain unfinished. The working party's main concern over the execution of the 'project' lay with the intensity of treatment given to the chosen topic. Here L. A. S. introduced the notion of 'thresholds' as a useful basis for guidance when choosing topics for project work. Any teaching course ought to consist of a number of major topics or themes which when linked together give the course its unity and coherence. These could be regarded as first threshold topics. They are then broken down into greater detail, the amount of detail varying with the nature of the topic or course and the abilities and interests of pupils and teachers. This breakdown provides further thresholds. An example of such a breakdown is to be found in Appendix 3. Experience of projects with 14–16 year olds suggests that it is extremely rare for a good project to be undertaken upon a first threshold topic and that too often topics at the second threshold turn out to be largely descriptive. The ideal 'project' should be based on a third threshold topic upon which evidence is available, and upon which questions can be asked and answers supplied.

Finally, the working party took the view that oral assessment of project work was essential. This would provide an opportunity to see what candidates had got out of the 'project' in terms of their understanding of their chosen topic and to display that understanding in a context wider than that provided by the project itself. The main difficulty here, as with all oral assessment, is the practical one of the time it takes, and much work, is needed upon moderation techniques involving sampling and the use of taped material.

The structure of the assessment having been decided the one outstanding matter still requiring decision was, 'What information should be given to schools?' It was suggested in Chapter 2 that a syllabus is a form of contract between school and board. On the basis of this analogy, what the working party had to decide was the kind of offer to make to schools when inviting them to take part in the project as partners in a joint enterprise. The offer that was eventually proposed was very simple. It consisted of three things, a title, the five aims and the structure of the assessment. This was to be accompanied by a gloss in which the working party set down in outline its thinking on the three parts of the offer. The composition of trial question papers and of the actual examination papers, which would inevitably contain a wide choice of questions, was to be determined by a consideration of the teaching syllabuses submitted by those taking part. The teachers would also be asked to contribute questions to a 'pool' from which, after validation, the question papers would be drawn. These proposals were accepted by the A.E.B. and issued in the form of a document entitled 'Pilot Project in the Assessment of World History at "O" level'. This document appears as Appendix 2 by kind permission of the A.E.B. When it was issued in September 1970 it constituted a unique Mode 1 'syllabus'. It was accompanied by a second document giving some example of questions that might be used in the assessment.

Such was the offer, made initially for two years; whether it would work in practice would depend upon the schools through their provision of teaching syllabuses and suggestions for questions, and upon the willingness of the A.E.B. to provide the resources necessary to maintain at least in the early stages a virtually continuous consultancy service. In the event both schools and board were not able to meet the challenge. The reasons for this, while understandable, need looking into, for unless these requirements can be met in the future then the model suggested by the project for co-operative curriculum/course development and evaluation within the framework of a national examination will remain theoretical rather than practical.

Why was the challenge not met, and why in consequence did the project in a number of respects become much more like a conventional Mode 1 with a modicum of teacher assessment thrown in? In what follows it is only fair to say that the authors are being wise after the event. They would also recognize that the amount of time and money that schools and examining boards, operating as they do at present, can devote to projects such as this must necessarily be limited. Nevertheless, it was a disappointment to the authors that those concerned in the project maintained traditional roles in the board/school dialogue.

There were two major reasons why the challenge was not met. First, there was the inability of almost all those participating to set down their teaching syllabuses in any systematic fashion. Secondly, there was the inadequacy, in terms of both quality and quantity, of the questions submitted for the 'pool'. These remarks and those that follow may seem unnecessarily, indeed unfairly, critical; such is not the intention. Experiments rarely work statisfactorily on the first occasion, and it is essential to learn from experience, particularly when, as was the case here, there was little or nothing from the past upon which to build. The participants, with one exception, produced not teaching syllabuses but rather examining syllabuses which were simply statements of content. Significantly, the exception was from the one technical college involved which proposed an integrated team teaching programme. Since both the production of teaching syllabuses and the question pool were key features in the development of the assessment, the nature of the schools' responses turned the A.E.B.'s role into a 'doing' rather than an 'advisory' one, and thus shifted the balance of power away from the schools to the board. This was a matter of some significance in a joint exercise which had difficulty in achieving equipoise, although probably no-one appreciated this at the time.

Until teachers can construct and set down teaching syllabuses for the benefit of people outside their own schools, then joint ventures which are genuinely joint are almost impossible. The basic reason for this inability or unwillingness is that in the past secondary school teachers have rarely had to set down syllabuses because public examinations have done it for them. The position is made worse, moreover, by the fact that the single subject tradition makes it more likely even today that experienced teachers will operate largely on their own rather than as part of a team. Large schools and integrated programmes are slowly breaking this practice down, but we should remind ourselves that both of these are still in a minority.

In the case of the world history project the situation would have been greatly improved if teachers from interested schools had been involved, without any commitment to participate, in the working party's discussions from the outset. This would not have been easy because of the way in which the project had started and because of the numbers involved, but it would have been invaluable. One of the weaknesses of the present external examination structure is that schools are presented with syllabuses in large measure on a take it or leave it basis. Whilst believing that it was doing something different the World History Project did exactly the same thing. The eighteen schools and one technical college who had agreed to take part in the project met the 'board' for the first time in November 1970, some two years after the working party's discussions had started. It was not surprising that this first meeting and much subsequent discussion was devoted to explaining the working party's thinking on issues such as the assessment of concepts and skills and over notions such as 'thresholds'. The working party and the board fell between two stools; they didn't involve the schools early enough, and having failed to do this they didn't provide enough explanation with the information that was eventually sent out. A systematic attempt, for example, to explain the matrix, or the issuing of sample syllabuses resulting from the use of the matrix would, in their different ways, have been helpful.

Inevitably, differences of opinion developed in the early meetings and the working party found itself on occasion fighting to maintain what it believed in. While this process was a marked improvement on the usual method of criticizing 'syllabuses', it was quite inimical to a joint exercise. For a joint exercise differences must be ironed out in advance so that those who proceed are united upon the underlying principles of what they are doing, and hence upon where they intend to arrive; differences can still remain about methods and routes. On occasion agreement to differ may be appropriate and realistic but it should be *agreement* to differ. Although the A.E.B. rapidly and sympathetically extended the opportunities for more informal communications by splitting up the participants into three largely geographically based groups or consortia with a member of the working party acting as convenor to each, this was done too late and ought to have been built in from the start. Such groupings also require full clerical and secretarial services from the board, and the importance of this fact took some time to be appreciated.

The result was that a number of compromises were reached and changes were made to the original scheme, one of which, again with hindsight, was most unfortunate. Certain features of the project, which were not fully revealed to most of the participants until after they had agreed to take part, were so new that a number of them had second thoughts. A desire to avoid withdrawals and to safeguard the interests of the candidates led the A.E.B. to allow those schools in the project which wished to do so to enter their pupils for both the project 'examination' and for the A.E.B.'s existing 'O' level syllabus 'Britain and World Affairs since 1870'. Any students doing this would be credited with their best performance. On the face of it this appeared to be to everyone's advantage. In practice the differences between the two examination programmes, both in emphasis (the existing A.E.B. syllabus was very 'British' orientated), and in methods of assessment (the existing examination made use solely of the traditional essay) meant that it was difficult to pursue both programmes successfully. In consequence schools were tempted to play safe and not commit themselves fully to the project.

The other major change introduced as a result of pressure from the participants was in the structure of the assessment. The weighting of the written paper was reduced from 65 per cent to 50 per cent and the resulting 15 per cent was given to the schools to assess the five aims in whatever way they thought best. This again seemed at first sight to be an improvement and to increase flexibility. In practice, however, a lack of preliminary discussion led in many cases to insufficient thought being given to the use of this portion of the assessment and its value was often very limited. In addition, of course, it posed further problems of comparability.

As already mentioned the second major reason why the challenge posed by the project was not met lay with the inadequate quality, range and number of questions submitted for the 'pool'. This underlined once again how little time most teachers devote to assessment in general and to the setting of questions in particular. It also underlined how demanding is the professional activity of setting questions. The working party had proposed the use of questions rather different from those found in current 'O' level history papers, in particular the kind of question to which the label 'structured'[1] is often applied. They had, however, supplied nothing more than examples as guidance for those who were expected to contribute questions to the 'pool'. The inadequacy of the response in view of the difficulties was thus hardly surprising. If a joint exercise of this kind hopes to obtain high quality questions then the examining board must provide teachers with both information and training as a matter of routine. Much more work should also be undertaken by the boards to establish question banks for the use of schools and teachers, rather than for their own use, An example of the kind of discussion paper upon the assessment of the five aims of the project which could have been issued to the participating schools as information is attached as Appendix 3.

Information and training alone will not guarantee quality, nor can one ensure that all who read the information or take part in the courses will subsequently set questions. Two things will inevitably happen, however,

---

[1] A structured question is one which gives pupils a certain amount of guidance as to possible lines which their answers might take. Those answering such a question are thus provided with a framework within which to work. The question itself will usually contain some information either in the form of written material or of diagrams, maps, pictures and the like.

and these of themselves justify the expenditure of time and money; first, all who participate will become more critical of the questions that they and others use and set, and will thus become more perceptive teachers. Secondly the basic platform of knowledge about assessment amongst teachers will be extended, and as a result formal training will be both enhanced and supplemented by informal, yet informed, activity in schools.

This brief analysis of the A.E.B. World History Project implies that the following requirements are essential if the model suggested by the project for co-operative curriculum course development and evaluation is to work.

1 Direct involvement of all likely participants at the very beginning of any project, scheme or idea.
2 Greater emphasis by all the agencies concerned with the pre-and in-service training of teachers upon practical curriculum-course development and evaluation.
3 The provision by examining boards, as a part of their routine work, of training services in respect of techniques and problems of assessment.
4 The development by examining boards of question banks for school and teacher use.
5 The willingness by teachers to devote more time to the developmental and evaluative aspects of their work.

Such basic requirements need more than will, time and money for their achievement. They need changes in attitudes by both teachers and examining boards. As the requirements are demanding for all concerned it is not surprising that for many the traditional roles are more comfortable. The pressures, however, are mounting, particularly with the growing development of integrated courses of study,[1] to find some acceptable middle way between the unique single school Mode 3 (for which incidentally there will always be a place and a need) and the completely external Mode 1. The slowly changing form of Mode 1 is sufficient evidence of the need for such a middle way. The pace of change in the external examining system, however, still does not match the pace of change in the curriculum, and hence it fails to meet the requirements of an increasing number of schools. These schools need the help of examining boards without their direction. This is why finding a worthwhile model for such a middle way is so important.

[1] Throughout this book great stress has been laid upon integrated courses, and many of the examples are taken from them rather than from history courses. This is only in part because the authors believe in integrated and inter-disciplinary curriculum/course developments and would like to see them extended. In part it is also because integrated courses give a particularly sharp edge to the problems of assessment and enable them to be considered untrammelled to a great extent by what has happened in the past.

The next chapter endeavours to provide some answers to the question 'What are the next steps?' Whatever may result, however, greater attention will have to be paid to the service functions of examining boards. Only if these are greatly increased in both extent and quality can teachers concentrate upon a key, although often neglected, part of their work, namely curriculum building and its evaluation through the assessment of the courses they develop.

CHAPTER SIX

A Strategy Emerges.
Potential Lines of Development

Where do we go from here? The problem that faces all externally examined and certificated courses is how to avoid interference with the curriculum and the courses devised by schools, and at the same time to establish and maintain nationally acceptable standards. In reality these are our old friends validity and reliability somewhat differently described, and, as always, it is essential that we ask which of the two is the more important. In 1973 the framework within which the external examination system in England and Wales operates is a multi-faceted one. At the risk of over simplification, it is reasonable to suggest that at the present time there are three basic variables: the number of schools; the nature of the curriculum and the courses which emerge from it; and the nature of the assessment provided. The number of schools taking any particular examination can range from one to several thousands. The curriculum and its resulting courses can be based upon a single discipline, or the individual disciplines can be totally submerged. The assessment can range from totally external to completely internal (albeit externally moderated), and it can employ a single assessment or a wide variety of techniques.

Within this framework the two principal agencies involved, the schools and examining boards, interact in a wide variety of ways both with each other and with other agencies as well, and produce in consequence versions of an interaction model. These are described as versions of the same model rather than as different models, because the basic problem remains the same regardless of numbers of schools or of curriculum or assessment patterns, and because the principal agencies are also the same. In this book so far we have really been looking at three versions of this model. The first is the traditional one through which Mode 1 is developed. We call this variety the 'association version'. Interaction between school and board does take place but it is on well defined and disciplined lines. C.S.E. opened the door to another version which is exemplified in this book by the Hedley Walter scheme. Here a single school puts a proposal to an examining board or boards, and after obtaining approval it constructs the assessment and plays a part in the processes leading to the award of grades by the board concerned. We call this the 'accommodation' version. The interaction in a proposal such as the Hedley Walter one is much less formal and far more frequent than in the first version, but the schools concerned have in the main to accommodate the requirements of the boards in order to achieve most of their aims. Despite the view held in certain quarters that Mode 3 is a free-wheeling exercise in which anything goes, the overwhelming majority of Mode 3s are processed rigorously through this version of the model. The third variety, which has been exemplified by the World History Project, we have called the 'collaborative' version. Here the interaction between schools and boards is on a much more equal footing and the restraints imposed by board upon school are both less apparent and less significant. It failed to develop, however, into an equal and natural partnership because of an imbalance in the work load and hence in the relationship between board and schools, which resulted from the inability of both to perceive and implement exactly what was required of them.

A consideration of these three versions would suggest that they become progressively more demanding for both schools and boards. This increased demand is principally in terms of expertise, flexibility and communications. The collaborative version requires, for example, much greater knowledge of practical curriculum development, of course construction and of techniques of assessment from the teachers, and a greater willingness to hammer out their requirements in a continuous dialogue than do the other two. Similarly it requires more in terms of consultancy and thus in terms of time, money and resources from the examining boards. Indeed it will almost certainly require a re-appraisal of the latter's role with consequential effects upon its structure, size and staffing. On occasions the expertise and resources cannot be provided from within either board or school, and the involvement of other agencies, for example the inspectorate, colleges of education and local authorities, is necessary. Flexibility in the context of public examinations is also bedevilled by the use that is made of examination results. The phrase 'the demands of society' can easily become a dead hand upon innovation although it is all too easy to create these very demands by appealing to them. There is no doubt that a more flexible curriculum requires the re-education not only of teachers and examining board staff but also of parents, users and employers. All this requires communications of a frequency, intensity and extent that have not hitherto been thought necessary in the domain of public examinations. This is a point to which further consideration will be given in the concluding chapter.

The return for all this hard work and cost lies in the emergence of a freer curriculum. Such a curriculum is not only related more closely to the needs of schools and thus more responsive to them, but is able to maintain that responsiveness through a continuing process of evaluation in which external examination can play a vital part. Equally important is the improvement in the quality of teaching that will result from more direct and deep involvement of teachers in curriculum and course planning, in assessment and in evaluation. It is very pertinent to ask, therefore, whether these three versions of the model can meet the present needs of curriculum and assessment in secondary schools, quite apart from coping with the future, or whether further versions will be necessary. The examples illustrated in the book have been fairly modest in curriculum terms; the Hedley Walter scheme was a straightforward integration of four subjects; an integration moreover in which the subject elements remained very recognizable in the assessment. The World History Project was based upon a single aspect of a very widely taught single subject, albeit a wide ranging one. They could thus be absorbed into the existing system without the need for reorganization or re-appraisal of procedures. The Hedley Walter scheme was in administrative terms another Mode 3 subject to the requirements of the two boards concerned. The World History Project was initiated by an examining board on the advice of an appointed working party, and was made available to a small group of selected schools. The assessment proposed in both schemes was not particularly innovatory, although this was far less true of the World History Project than of the Hedley Walter scheme.

It seems reasonable to suggest, therefore, that, provided the requirements which emerged from a consideration of the World History Project are met in full, the collaborative version of the model is capable of meeting the demands which will result from initiatives like the Hedley Walter scheme (including the overwhelming majority of Mode 3s) and from the introduction into the curriculum of new aspects of existing subjects or new subjects intitiated by examining boards. In saying this one must not undervalue the achievement of realizing these requirements in practice nor underestimate the efforts that will be needed from a wide range of agencies. There is a very long way to go before something like the World History Project realizes its full potential as a collaborative curriculum/ course development exercise. There is a very long way to go before the majority of teachers have the quality of experience and expertise to enable them to devise individual and group Mode 3s which will make a real contribution to the curriculum; and to enable them to introduce a wide range of assessment practices. There is also a very long way to go before examining boards are able to provide the necessary consultancy services both in terms of quality and quantity to assist and stimulate schools to make that contribution. However, the structure for 'coping' seems to be available, if the will, the time and the resources are devoted to its establishment and maintenance.

There is more, however, to curriculum development at the present time than integration in the social sciences and the introduction of world history. There are, for example, the courses that L. A. S. and the Goldsmiths' Curriculum Laboratory assumed would emerge and encouraged to emerge from a wide variety of single school or group initiatives. These in their turn will make new demands upon assessment. Can the procedures outlined for the collaborative version and the suggestions made for its improvement cater for developments such as these? The first step to answering this question is to have a look at Inter-disciplinary Enquiry (I.D.E.) which has only been briefly defined so far in this book. I.D.E. is not chosen because it is typical, but because it is the 'sharp edge of the chisel' of educational development. If a version of the interaction model can accommodate I.D.E. then it is reasonable to assume that it can accommodate anything else that is going on in terms of curriculum development and assessment practice in secondary schools at the present time.

As mentioned in Chapter 3, enquiry is the central pillar of the so-called Fourfold Curriculum,[1] and I.D.E. is one of the components. I.D.E. as an approach to learning, contrary to what many teachers believe, does not constitute a threat to the disciplined study of subjects. It does, however, permit schools to mount studies which are not offered and would be very difficult to offer, by schools which work totally within the framework of a subject-based curriculum. Through the emphasis it gives to both individual and group study and activities, it can stimulate the development of real collaborative learning by teacher and taught, and can do much to promote communication skills. It is not, however, something which can be borrowed and used like curriculum materials or a new text book. It has to be worked for and worked towards and this can often be a slow and frustrating process.

The activities which are undertaken by teachers and students during an I.D.E. programme normally have their starting points in a theme, and are developed under the umbrella of the theme in different ways as different sets of criteria are applied to them. There are literally thousands of themes that can be suggested, and there are thousands of ways in which they can be treated. By way of illustration one hundred themes under four general headings are provided in Appendix 4. The four headings are as follows:

1 Living in a contemporary world
2 Man

[1] See bibliography for a list of publications on I.D.E.

3 The processes we employ
4 Wonderment

Certain features of these hundred themes and of any other list of themes warrant further attention. First of all none of them is new, many have promoted a great deal of interesting work in schools in integrated and inter-disciplinary programmes as well as in subject-based courses. Secondly, many of them interrelate, although the nature of the interrelationships depends both upon the individual and upon the standpoints from which the themes are viewed. Thirdly the themes in terms of their 'thresholds' (a notion which was explained in chapter 5) can be classified in different ways by the application of different criteria.

The appeal of a theme to an individual very often determines the extent to which it is developed in terms of its educational outcomes. Some teachers find it easier than others to take a synoptic view of the potential of several themes considered together, while others see more readily the potential for developing courses based upon a single theme.

Once teachers find a flow of ideas emanating from a theme or group of themes, then they are in a position to develop, first of all, a programme of study which includes the strategies for tackling the flow, secondly schemes of work emerging from that programme and thirdly (if they wish) proposals for assessment. (In this connection it is important to stress that I.D.E. will almost certainly have started in those schools which decide to adopt it in the early years of secondary education if not before.) Each of these three stages starts with a roughly drawn outline which then is subject to closer analysis and elaborated in more detail. In developing the programme of study use might be made of a conceptual map or of the matrix.[1] The elaboration of the schemes of study means consideration of different teaching strategies and of resource requirements. Proposals for assessment need a more detailed consideration of the subjects which might be involved in the programme after it has been amplified through the courses of study. The identification of subjects (as can be seen in Appendix 1) was at the heart of L. A. S.'s original proposals for the external assessment of I.D.E. His initial attempts in this direction were based upon the vast theme 'Living in a technological society'. In retrospect its very size made it an unlikely starter and almost certainly contributed to the failure described in chapter 3. Nevertheless its possibilities were also vast and it would have been (and still is) perfectly possible to develop it in such a way that it could occupy virtually all a student's weekly timetable over a period of two or three years. The range of subjects that could emerge from the study of such a theme could include moreover all those at present covered

[1] See Chapter 5.

in a normal secondary curriculum, and more besides. Other themes and different methods of treatment would produce different lists of subjects.

One such theme was the title of World History Project itself, 'World Powers and World Events in the Twentieth Century', which would have been much more manageable than 'Living in a technological society'. An I.D.E. programme based upon it could have included in subject terms, history, economics, geography and English usage. Other programmes based on the theme might have developed in rather different directions and chosen contemporary literature, religious studies and general science as being relevant subjects emerging from the particular treatment given to it. In the event only the one technical college involved in the first year of the project considered an integrated approach of any kind, and this was not I.D.E.

The significant point of difference between an I.D.E. assessment scheme and that adopted by the Hedley Walter school was that the latter identified the same four subjects for all students and asked for certification in only those. An assessed I.D.E. programme would permit students to make different choices from a predetermined array of subjects upon which the examining board would have been asked to provide certification. Any school therefore which asks to have an I.D.E. programme externally assessed, whether on its own or in association with other schools upon a common theme, should do three things. First it should set down its version of how it interprets the theme. This establishes the framework of the programme in a way which can be contrasted with the curriculum and courses which it replaces and thus permits the statement of the array of subjects upon which assessment will be provided. Secondly, within that framework, individuals should make their subject choices from the array. There will almost certainly be some restrictions upon that choice, more usually upon the maximum number of subjects that can be chosen, but on occasion it might also be necessary to enter all students for one subject—English for example —because of pressures from outside the school. Thirdly, having made this choice, the studies in depth undertaken by the students should be related to the subjects chosen in order to provide the relevant evidence for assessment. These suggestions are a great deal easier to describe than to undertake, particularly as they have not as yet been applied to an actual I.D.E. programme. 'Living in a technological society' never got off the ground and the World History Project was not interpreted as the basis for a potential I.D.E. programme by those involved. Most of the remainder of this chapter will therefore be devoted to looking at these suggestions for an assessment strategy in respect of three possible I.D.E. programmes developed from themes provided in Appendix 4. The results will then be related to the collaborative version of the interaction model to see whether it can meet the demands as it stands or whether and in what respects it needs to be modified.

The authors are very conscious of the fact that in describing these three programmes and indeed in providing the rather formidable list of one hundred themes in the appendix they are treading on unfamiliar ground which may prove daunting to many teachers. The need to tread on unfamiliar ground is desirable because it is only by going to the coal face that real progress can be made. Much, therefore, of what is said in this book and of what will be carried out in practice in the next few years in relation to the joint development of curriculum and assessment must be tentative. This tentativeness will slowly disappear as modifications are introduced following practical validation of schemes by those involved. In the early stages, however, things will be said and done which are 'old hat' to a few and anathema to many others.

Example 1   An approach using a major concern as a theme
For the first example the theme 'Women are people too' has been chosen. As will be seen from the themes presented in Appendix 4 this appeared at the end of the list devoted to 'Man' the rest of which all start with the word 'Man'. It might thus appear that 'Women are people too' was an afterthought from two married men as a sop to Women's Lib! Far from being an afterthought this particular theme has been promoted by one of the authors (L. A. S.) at conferences concerned with integrated studies and inter-disciplinary enquiry for many years. It has moreover never failed to arouse widespread interest on these occasions as a possible basis for a curriculum programme. It is couched in terms which focus on a 'concern' which is controversial, contemporary—albeit with a long history—and both public in the sense that it has for years been well articulated through the media and individually personal to both men and women whatever their age. Because it possesses these features it is likely to be seen as a theme which can sponsor a wide-ranging experience in inter-disciplinary enquiry.

A preliminary scrutiny of the theme can produce a number of purely traditional areas for investigation, but it can in addition offer to students possible lines of study which are different if not new. As phrased, the title emphasizes in a polemic, indeed provocative way, the historical truth that women have tended to be viewed by both sexes as being members of a 'man's world'. It thus provides the opportunity for studies which investigate the reasons and justification for such an assumption. Other areas of interest which might be suggested by the theme are as follows: women viewed within the context of various religions from the standpoint of both the beliefs and 'religious practices'; women as viewed and portrayed by poets, dramatists and writers; male and female, the basic application of the principle of division of labour (this can either be considered historically, in relation to the present day or in terms of the future); women, the home-makers; women, the basic educators; the notion of 'family'—'nuclear' and 'extended' with comparisons between 'family' and 'tribe'; women and the notion of 'ownership' in various contexts and settings; the role of women as portrayed by custom, tradition and convention, and their relationship to men within these contexts; women as seen through the eyes of men, and women's views on the ways they feel that they are viewed by men; spinsterhood, marriage, courtship, divorce, monogamy, polygamy, motherhood, apparent or real enslavement; women and employment including that short period of history when 'a woman's place is in the home' became 'largely accepted' by both men and women; women's organizations, societies, sub-cultures, and women within the context of sub-cultures dominated (for various 'reasons') by men; widowhood—real and 'grass'; women's rights movements in various parts of the world viewed against the background of events largely dominated by men; women as consumers; women in industrial/technological employment as compared with women in basically agricultural economies; women as pioneers in various fields of endeavour; women in war; women and decision-making; females within demographical studies; females within various cultures; and so on. The possibilities are limitless.

Added to and suitably developed this list of possible areas of interest within the theme embraces some orthodox subjects within current secondary curricula, for example: biology, especially human biology, economic and social history, political, in particular constitutional history both national and comparative, sociology, comparative religious studies, literature and, because of the very nature of the studies, expressive arts, particularly language (mother tongue). In addition many areas of study emerging from the theme could be grouped under the title of social studies and thereby provide opportunities for some 'newcomers' to the secondary curriculum to find a place within a school's programme. These should include, for example, various aspects of health education, careers education, money management, legal studies, child care (perhaps allied to community education), community studies and moral education. Additionally programmes emerging from the theme could provide opportunities for subjects which are already an autonomous part of the curriculum to make further relevant and useful contributions, for example mathematics (including statistics), domestic science, foreign languages, geography and business studies. Thus an I.D.E. programme on such a theme could be seen as crucial to a school's curriculum in that it would help to create bridges for both students and teachers between different areas of study. This appears to the authors to constitute a marked advance in educational practice which takes but rarely a synoptic view of the curriculum and in which the relationships between a series of disparate studies are rarely made explicit to the students taking them. But this is a matter of opinion.

How could programmes such as those envisaged above be developed so that they could be certified by an external examining board? If answers cannot be found to this question then a substantial number of teachers who might like to approach orthodox studies in unorthodox ways without necessarily being committed to I.D.E. will not do so for fear of putting their students at risk. If this happens then the curriculum will remain in a rut.

The keys for making an I.D.E. programme of proposed study (and indeed any programme) assessable are rigour and definition. These may appear to some to be incompatible with the ethos of I.D.E., but this is far from the case. Integrated and inter-disicplinary work is in many cases sloppy, and it is often forgotten that education which is ostensibly more open and unorthodox requires a great deal more underpinning in terms of thought and action than that which is more orthodox and closed. Rigour here means rigour in analysis. This results in definition, not in the sense that everyone on a given day or given week is doing the same thing, but in the sense that all parties to the assessment of a particular course—students, teachers and examining boards—have a yardstick against which to evaluate its outcomes.

The rigorous analysis must be applied first of all to the educational objectives of the programme. These should then be made explicit in course outlines, which are roughly drawn at first and then, as suggested earlier in this chapter, are made more detailed. The resulting broad areas of investigation are changed finally into specific schemes of work. Such a process requires thorough analysis of the relevant learning situations and resources to enable students to gain the maximum value from their work. It also requires detailed consideration of the subject areas which might fall within the course outlines and hence might be exemplified in individual students' schemes of work.

The interrelationship between objectives and the educational approaches adopted is, as always, crucial. It should, of course, determine in large measure the patterns of assessment adopted but it also greatly influences teachers' decisions as to whether to adopt an I.D.E., integrated or single subject programme. Decisions here in their turn help to determine the subject areas to be included in any proposals made to an examining board for certification.

Let us now look in more detail at the theme 'Women are people too' and see how a two year I.D.E. programme based upon it could be assessed. In what follows three assumptions are made. First, that the programme is developed by a single school although it could just as easily be developed by a group of schools in collaboration. Secondly, that the two years referred to are the last two years of compulsory secondary education, that is to say at present it will involve students in the 14–16 year old age range. Thirdly, that the decision to have the programme externally assessed has resulted from a detailed debate of the issues involved. This decision is thus built into the preliminary planning.

No group of teachers will embark on any I.D.E. programme without a great deal of forward planning. It is, moreover, almost certain that schools deciding to develop an assessable programme will have had past experience of I.D.E. work lower down the school. During the course of this preparatory work the teachers concerned will have rehearsed in some detail the potential of the theme as they see it, and considered a variety of ways in which it might be realized in terms of actual courses. This should lead, as has already been suggested, to a flexible organizational structure capable of containing a variety of instructional and learning approaches. Students will be involved in exercises in group work and individual study with a small team of teachers. Because of the nature of the enquiry processes involved both teachers and students are likely to meet for relatively lengthy blocks of time during a single week. The amount of 'blocked time' at any stage of a course will depend largely upon the scope and intensity of treatment given to particular aspects of it. This may not always reveal itself until the course is under way and it will not necessarily be the same for all students. Flexibility is thus essential. Indeed it is possible to envisage the allocation of time as a variable over the two year period, either being extended progressively for all students over the period as a whole, or being varied for individual students in any number of ways throughout the period.

However careful the preparation it is unlikely that the first six months of any courses that may be developed will provide an agreed basis for external assessment. However, the groundwork must be done by establishing first of all the parameters in subject terms for the programme as a whole, and secondly, to start to establish these same parameters for each individual student's courses of study. At the end of this preliminary period for which six months is suggested, an approach should be made to the examining board with which the school is already or wishes to be associated. The timing of this first approach is vital. It must be made in sufficient time to enable agreement to be reached for certification at the end of the second year. It cannot on the other hand be made before the students have had the chance to appreciate the various lines of development and enquiry open to them within the theme, and to look at the opportunities that these provide for 'in depth' studies. The school's proposals to the board at this first approach consist of as detailed a statement as possible of the likely lines of study that the theme will promote and the linkages that it sees existing between these lines of study and named subjects. It is thus very different from the approach that a school wishing to secure approval of a Mode 3 would make at the present time. It is different primarily because it is essentially tentative and not specific. It does not ask for certification in 'n' named subjects which all students will take and which will be assessed in an agreed fashion. Instead it asks the examining board to provide certification upon an agreed list of subjects without any firm commitment as to which students will take which subjects and without details of the specific assessment patterns to be adopted. Agreement should, however, be reached—assuming, of course, that all goes well—upon the maximum number of subjects which any one student will be allowed to take for assessment purposes. This decision would normally be related to the amount of time the I.D.E. programme occupies in the school timetable. Agreement should also be reached upon the broad framework of assessment which in relation to an I.D.E. programme is likely to be largely continuous, based upon students' individual or group studies. This does not preclude the subsequent use of formal tests but these, as will be seen later, are more likely to emerge as the course develops rather than be built in from the start. The board's reply is also essentially tentative. It does not give instant decisions for or against but rather initiates a continuous dialogue which will lead to a series of decisions spread over a period of time. The first of these decisions relates to the array of subjects for which certification will be provided.

An I.D.E. programme based on the theme 'Women are people too' could legitimately ask for certification and provide supporting evidence to justify the claim upon the following eight subjects: human biology, economic and social history, political history, sociology, religious studies, literature, English language, and social studies (or social education, which is possibly a better title for the studies that are likely to be involved). It might be agreed that five of these will be the maximum upon which any one student can be certificated. The number of subjects assessed could thus range from one to five according to the degree and nature of the involvement of the individual student in the programme.

Armed with this agreement (for which, it must be stressed, the school has had to argue on the basis of carefully thought through proposals) the school can now turn its attention to the development of programmes of study for the individual students. In the first six months of the two year programme most students will be considering and planning their studies in depth. For those students, however, who have enjoyed several years of I.D.E., work on these studies will have already begun and this work will have been used by both teachers and students as part of the ongoing assessment that is undertaken throughout any I.D.E. programme. After agreement has been reached on the array of subjects for certification, the students, in conjunction with their teachers, will begin to reduce the range of their studies and to provide themselves with a frame of reference for their work which will take account of their interests and abilities. This 'paring down' also increasingly takes account of the subjects available for certification, so that by the end of the first year of the course, the students in-depth studies become their passports for entry to subjects chosen from among the array. The gradual process of selection and refinement is not haphazard, but is guided throughout by teachers. It is about at this half way stage of the two year programme that the school, which has been in constant contact with the board, again approaches it formally, this time with an outline of the assessment patterns proposed for all the students involved, based upon studies in depth. These proposals relate to particular selected groupings of subjects, but are still tentative in that the students are not yet committed to any examination entry. It is at this stage also that the board will begin to offer specific advice about the limitations of individual programmes of work, and may suggest that further studies are necessary if a particular student expects to be certified in a particular subject. The board will also start to introduce its moderating procedures in respect of the work being undertaken. It will, of course, have been aware from the time of original submission that the general pattern of assessment is to be continuous and based largely upon individual and group studies. It should thus have laid the groundwork for moderation. It can now begin to spell out its proposals here as specific requirements in relation to such matters as visits by external moderators or the amount of work necessary for sampling purposes. There are in current use by examining boards a variety of approaches to the moderation of continuous assessment, and school and board in consultation will need to decide upon and use the most appropriate methods always bearing in mind the objectives of the programme.[1]

With six months of the course to go the school must now make its third and final specific approach to the board, although again the continuous nature of the dialogue should have been maintained. The school should now make a specific commitment for each student to enter 'n' named subjects chosen from the array. In the light of this the board will advise the school on the extent to which each student is or is not on target in terms of his or her studies. Where students are clearly falling short, then

---

[1] This important topic and the issues involved cannot be dealt with in this book. The interested reader is therefore referred to the Bibliography and in particular to *Techniques and Problems of Assessment* ed. H. G. Macintosh (Edward Arnold 1974) and to J.M.B. Occasional Publications Nos. 22, 26, 27 and 31.

discussion should take place on the evidence required to meet the shortfall. Under extreme conditions lack of evidence might require the Board to produce a test or tests so that the students concerned can show their levels of mastery of the skills, or their levels of understanding of the concepts, which their programmes have failed to reveal. Although in general I.D.E. programmes lend themselves to individual work and continuous assessment, the school itself might on occasion decide to use written tests and should be in a position to obtain those which it cannot construct itself from the board.

There is one particular aspect of any I.D.E. programme which might with advantage be assessed in a different way from the rest, and that is English language or, as it might more appropriately be called, English usage. As was mentioned earlier in the book, I.D.E. has the potential for helping students to master communication skills. Although there are plenty of opportunities throughout the entire programme for students to demonstrate their oral fluency and their facility in written communication, these skills can and probably should be evaluated in addition by means of a specially designed assessment. Part of this assessment would be continuous, but part would be terminal. Here again the examining board should be in a position to help.

Such is a possible way of assessing an I.D.E. programme based upon a theme. As this account shows the respective roles of schools and examining board differ markedly from those they adopt for more traditional subject-based assessment. The demands put upon both are also greatly extended. Before, however, considering whether the third or collaborative version of the interaction model, as it emerged from the consideration of the World History Project in Chapter 5, could stand up to such demands, we will look at two further and rather different approaches to an I.D.E. programme. One of these, a B.B.C. radio programme, is currently being assessed on a single subject basis by a G.C.E. board, and the other is but an idea for a programme, although one whose key concept is used in other more traditional courses of study many of which are assessed at the present time.

'Women are people too' as a theme is content orientated and can lead readily to subject based courses which are susceptible of external assessment and certification using the strategies acquired during earlier I.D.E. experiences. The B.B.C. course 'Living decisions' (our second example) illustrates the use of I.D.E. as a process of enquiry, which can be developed in a wide variety of courses. This use of I.D.E. as a kind of strategy of study is illustrated even more pointedly in the third example based on the concept 'Growth and decay'. In both these programmes it is most unlikely that the emergence of traditional subjects for assessment purposes will be other than a lengthy and indirect developmental process. Conversely it is equally unlikely that the concepts of 'Living Decisions' and 'Growth and Decay' will ever form the basis of assessed courses named after them. In the case of the B.B.C. programme, decision making as a strategy is assessed in practice within a course certificated as Family and Community Studies. With 'Growth and decay' the concept may well remain hidden as a basic strategy of study in largely traditional history or biology courses. Whether the concepts remain implicit or explicit however does not and must not alter the requirements necessary for assessment.

Example 2   An approach using a process of enquiry as a theme
This example concerns an interesting initiative taken by the B.B.C. Just prior to the establishment in 1970 of the Open University, the B.B.C., through its Further Education Department, ran a series of three 'Gateway Courses'; 'Reading to Learn', 'Square Two' and 'Man in Society'. They were designed to provide adults who were considering enrolling for courses at the Open University with experience of the kind of tuition they could expect to receive. The three courses, therefore, combined in different ways instruction on radio and television together with course books and other recommended reading. Additional support was also provided for those who wanted it by a correspondence course and by part-time courses run in conjunction with the programmes by a number of technical colleges. The A.E.B., largely as a result of its interest in mature students, undertook to provide information about performance on the courses for those who wanted it. This association was to lead to further collaboration between the B.B.C. and the A.E.B. of a much more significant kind in relation to an adult learning project which went on the air in the autumn of 1973 under the title 'Living Decisions in Family and Community': the two authors were involved in various aspects of the preliminary work for this course. The significance of this collaboration lay in the fact that it marked a further extension of the concept of co-operation between the two fields of curriculum and assessment development, this time involving not schools but a national institution. As with the earlier 'Gateway Courses' the radio series 'Living Decisions' was supported by a course book. This time, however, the supporting services were more extensive and more deliberately developed. Advice and guidance were built into the course; all the major correspondence colleges were encouraged by the B.B.C. to provide courses and considerable help was given to technical colleges in various parts of the British Isles which wished to run courses in conjunction with the broadcasts. The assessment provided by the A.E.B., although still an optional extra, was also significantly different in that it formed part of the national examining system and awarded the successful student an 'O' level in Family and Community Studies.

Michael Stephens, the Head of Further Education (Radio) B.B.C. described the development and nature of the new project in the following words:[1]

There began in the autumn of 1970 a series of meetings between B.B.C. staff and external consultants drawn from the worlds of adult and further education, curriculum development, educational publishing and examining boards. The first question that had to be resolved was what would be the most appropriate 'subject' for the course; and here we immediately faced a real dilemma. If the resulting qualification was going to have any educational credibility it had to be 'in' something, had to sit relatively easily alongside, for example, an 'O' level in English or in Maths; and if the course and its participating students were going to get the support we hoped from other agencies of adult and further education, it must be identifiable to them as having at least a strong affinity with a recognised area of learning. But if, on the other hand, it was going to attract and serve as well adults unsure of their own learning potential and so reluctant to join adult education classes, and encourage them to take steps to further their own education more actively, then it must be related more to their experience of living than to an academic idea of learning ... we decided to apply a series of specific tests to the 'subject' that had been tentatively suggested. This—somewhat ironically because we were involved in the process—was 'decision making', but as a personal rather than an institutional activity.

Although the B.B.C. project was designed for adults it should be stressed that the ideas behind it are also particularly relevant for students in the last two or three years of secondary education.

Stephens went on to say:

And so, to cut a long story short, we eventually emerged with the proposition that we should offer a course in 'Living Decisions in Family and Community' based on a syllabus that could bring the adult student to an 'O' level in Family and Community Studies ... The A.E.B. indicated a willingness which has recently been substantiated, to certificate a syllabus in family and community studies at (alternative) 'O' level ... It remains to be proved, of course that an 'O' level qualification in family and community studies will be acceptable in the employers' and educationists' worlds as a meaningful certificate of capacity and potential.

This account reinforces two major facets of the process that is involved

[1] *New B.B.C. Adult Learning Project.* Article by Michael Stephens in *Ideas*, No. 24, Jan., 1973.

D

when a school or other agency tries to gain recognition in terms of external certification for an obviously worthwhile educational activity. First that any proposal should be so phrased as to have meaning through linkage with existing recognised areas of study. Secondly, that the acceptance of a proposal by an examining board and the granting of certification does not of itself guarantee acceptability. This depends to a considerable extent upon the attitudes, unfortunately not always based upon proper evaluation of those who use the certificates. They inevitably have not been involved in the processes which led to its development. This is, of course, no new phenomenon. Certain G.C.E. subjects, notably in craft areas, assessed under Mode 1 arrangements, have not in the past proved acceptable to some agencies. It should be stressed, however, that the recent history of the introduction of new subjects into the examining system has been much more encouraging, and it is not long before the one-time newcomer is being used as an element of the criterion used for the evaluation of 'later newcomers'.

The work on the B.B.C. project revealed clearly to the authors the problems associated with promoting an examination on an I.D.E. programme based upon a process of enquiry. Tackled in the way described by Michael Stephens the outcome is single-subject certification, although the central nature of the process makes it capable of being used in a wide range of studies. The example is thus limited although its potential is considerable. For schools which wish to pursue the matter beyond single-subject certification there are two lines of development worth exploring. First, a number of processes, for example decision making, predictions, forecasting, extrapolation, trends, measurement and evaluation, and division of labour, can be drawn together for the purpose of developing pupils' skills in their use within the context of one or more traditional subjects. The resulting schemes of work and any assessment patterns adopted emphasize these processes, although the title of the subject being certificated would be a familiar one. The same technique of drawing together a number of processes and then developing an 'in depth' understanding of them through usage can be undertaken within the context of an I.D.E. programme based on a theme such as 'Confrontations in the comtemporary world' or within integrated studies programmes based, for example, on design or the humanities. Here assessment and certification can either be related to a single subject as with the B.B.C. course, or would develop on the lines suggested in the first example. Whatever line is adopted it would appear that processes such as decision making are not likely to find an easy place within the external system unless teachers can find ways of incorporating them—almost as if they were glue—within schemes of work which can offer to the examining boards and to those who accept their certificates recognizable areas of knowledge. Although this must sound like a note to hasten slowly or at least to hasten stealthily on this front, it must be added that the more extensively teachers accept the validity of emphasizing processes in learning and processes in living within their teaching programmes then the more quickly these same processes will gain recognition through external certification.

Example 3   An approach using a key concept as a theme
For the third example the key concept of 'Growth and Decay' has been chosen. The word 'key', of course, involves a value judgement, and a concept is only 'key' to those who believe it to be so. As with 'Living Decisions' it is not envisaged that the study of a programme based on this theme would lead to an 'O' level or C.S.E. with the same title. The concept can be used rather as strategy of study to build in extra dimensions to a student's work, and thus act as a stimulus to educational activity within a variety of courses, some of which might lead to single-subject certification. Some areas of study which might emerge from the practical application of 'the concept' in this way are:

1 Growth in time and space
2 The quality of growth
3 Forms of growth
4 Causes of growth
5 Effects of growth
6 The processes of growth
7 The perception of growth
8 The measurement of growth
9 The process of analysing growth
10 Attitude towards growth.

A similar list could be prepared for 'decay'. There is no significance incidentally in the order in which these are listed nor is there any uniformly correct way of applying them. Their value, relevance, relative importance and hence their ordering varies not only from topic to topic but from individual to individual. Within studies suggested by such a framework, examples of increasing complexity can be used as students feel their way towards an understanding of the concept and its transfer potential.

It is likely, as was suggested earlier, that such studies will lead to the use of other concepts, some of which will be contained in the list of suggested themes in 'The processes we employ' series in Appendix 4. Possible examples are: obsolescence, adaptability, evolution, measurement and evaluation, predictions, forecasting and extrapolation. The introduction of such further concepts must inevitably widen the scope of any studies which were originally started under the umbrella of 'Growth and Decay', and thus point to ways in which integrated or inter-disciplinary programmes can be developed, if required, to the point of external assessment. If, for example, a programme makes use of all or some of the additional concepts listed earlier in this paragraph then it is possible to see the emergence of a biological emphasis in the consideration of 'Growth and Decay'. It is equally possible, however, to introduce and involve concepts such as: freedom, law and order, convention, customs and traditions, ownership, division of labour and mobility. A theme such as 'Towards world government' can then be introduced as a means of exemplifying 'Growth and Decay'. Should developments in these directions take place then they would introduce legal, moral, historical, political and economic emphases.

The coverage of any of these named subject areas would not of course normally replicate or even approach the coverage provided by equivalent examining board syllabuses. Indeed, a coverage of this kind would not be seen as a high priority in an I.D.E. programme based on this theme; it would emerge rather as a by-product of the way in which the programme has developed. If, however it was decided to assess a programme based upon 'Growth and Decay', involving certification in one or several subjects, rather than use it as a strategy of study, then the same approach as that suggested for 'Women are people too' would have to be adopted. Securing agreement upon these subjects would be more difficult, however, and the planning of the resulting courses would be a longer and harder process.

The three examples (which grow progressively more complex in their demands) have all contained suggestions as to how they might be externally assessed and certificated. These are very much in outline; only in relation to 'Women are people too', much the simplest in this respect, has an attempt been made to expand the detail significantly and to propose a series of specific steps. Consideration of these steps seems to suggest that even if the requirements put forward in Chapter 5 as being essential to the working of the collaborative model were met in full the model would be inadequate to meet the demands placed upon it by I.D.E. programmes. These demands differ from those relating to the World History Project in respect of the extent and intensity of the interaction, and are brought about largely as a result of the non-subject basis of the I.D.E. programmes. This requires the subject elements, if they are going to emerge for assessment purposes, to emerge through the gradual development and expansion of the courses of study which flow out from the programme. These differences are further accentuated by the essentially external nature of the assessment proposed for the World History Project. Once the schools' teaching syllabuses for the project had been produced, contact between board and school remained at a relatively low level, mainly concerning itself with the schools contributions to the question pool, until the time when the board came to mark and moderate. Such a situation could not possibly obtain with an I.D.E. programme where a series of initiatives and decisions are necessary over a period of eighteen months to two years. Continuous interaction is vital here, as an extremely fluid pattern of development gradually settles down and in so doing provides the framework for assessment, which under the circumstances can only be continuous.

This need for continuous interaction suggests that the requirements previously considered to be adequate for the success of the collaborative version will fall short in relation to I.D.E. programmes in two respects. First, they do not lay sufficient emphasis upon the need for communications that are more extensive, continuous and demanding than anything previously considered necessary by either schools or examining boards. This aspect will be treated in some detail in the last chapter. Secondly, the requirements do not emphasize sufficiently the need for boards to service local groups of schools on a continuous basis. It is from such local groups or single schools that almost all I.D.E. programmes are likely to originate. Both these points impinge once again upon the structure of examining boards and thus upon their size and staffing; they also have significant implications for school organization and staffing.

It could be argued that these two points are in fact subsumed within the requirements set down in Chapter 5. In other words they are not additional requirements but rather an extension of those already noted and whose limitations have been exposed as a result of pressure. If this is considered a legitimate line of argument then the collaborative version of the interaction model should suffice provided it is given a much more powerful engine and a larger fuel supply. If not then a fourth version of the model needs to be developed perhaps called the 'intensive or sustained' version. Here jargon would appear to be getting the upper hand. Provided it is realized that the demands of assessed and certificated I.D.E. programmes are more intense and more continuous than those relating to assessed single-subject programmes, then the essential point has been appreciated and the relevant action can be taken to strengthen the model. The dividing line between a new requirement and an extension of an old one is blurred and such distinctions are not worth pursuing here.

CHAPTER SEVEN

The Future

Personal experiences such as those described in this book are unique, and it is pertinent to ask in this concluding chapter whether they have transfer-potential. Put in another way, is the approach suggested by the authors one that is likely to commend itself in practice to those who teach and to those who work for examining boards and other relevant agencies in the education serivce? The authors see no reason why it should not do so. They do not consider the general lines of their own experiences to be isolated ones, and they believe that an increasing number of teachers are coming to recognize that the existing fragmentation of curriculum development and assessment practice is to the disadvantage of both. In consequence there is a growing commitment to the concept of a structure which would permit the kind of continuous interaction between the agencies concerned which the authors advocate.

It is, however, arguable that this book, by its concentration on I.D.E. programmes and integrated courses and ways to assess them, has failed to put its message across in a form which reflects the realities faced by most teachers. The authors would, however, justify their emphasis on I.D.E. and integration on a number of grounds. First, a study of the most ad-vanced developments in any area enables one to identify more clearly the dimensions of problems in that same area. This makes it more likely that the solutions suggested will work under less extreme conditions. Secondly, there is no doubt that one of the major trends in curriculum development at the secondary level at the present time is towards integration. This is paralleled in instructional strategies by developments in self-paced learning. Assessment practice has to take account of such trends. Thirdly, I.D.E. as a concept has been badly misunderstood by many teachers in the past largely because they have envisaged it as an all-out attack on the subject based approach to curriculum development. Other teachers, who are sympathetic towards its aims, have neglected it because it has seemed to be unassessable in any formal sense. Both these tendencies have caused teachers to neglect the possibilities of its development within single sub-jects, and indeed on occasion to fail to appreciate that some of the things they are already doing in their curriculum are I.D.E.

Nevertheless, a teacher in any school or college begins development in any area from his or her existing position. For most this means a subject-based curriculum. Therefore this concluding chapter is concerned with finding ways and means for all teachers to move towards a freer curriculum as they see it rather than as others see it for them. One vital ingredient in any joint operation, however large or small, is a first class communications network. In the context of curriculum development in this country such a network does exist, but is remarkably diffuse and informal, involving agencies like the Schools Council, the Inspectorate, Local Education Authorities, Advisers and Teachers' Centres. The varied nature of the sources from which information and advice about educational matters can be obtained has often been regarded as a source of potential strength; the authors strongly disagree with this view. They regard it rather as a source of potential weakness. It results in schools and teachers spending far too much time on the mechanics of communicating and far too little time in discussing the results of the contacts they make through these communications. Not only is valuable information often missed but information which is obtained is often too fragmentary to be of much use. The authors argue that since curriculum development and its evaluation are integral activities, one of the most potent seed-beds for a freer curriculum at the secondary level lies in the interplay between examining board and schools. Therefore the principal agencies in a communications network relating to curriculum and assessment development should be examining boards (at present at the secondary level this means the G.C.E. and C.S.E. boards) with the remaining agencies acting as feeders and providing valuable supporting services upon request. There are two additional practical reasons for this suggestion. First that in embryo such a network already exists within and between examining boards, and secondly that the boards represent the one relatively stable element in the interaction model which this book has put forward. Schools disappear and re-emerge, the curriculum changes and assessment practices vary and develop; the boards, however, remain essentially the same. They ought, therefore, to become the hub of the wheel.

The kind of communications network here would be much wider than that which examining boards or any of the other agencies mentioned possess at present. Unlike those in use now, it would not be concerned exclusively with dealing with problems as they arise. At present communications mean such things as letters, talks, visits and discussions. Instead, the principal concerns would lie with information storage, retrieval, and dissemination. This too would require letters, talks, visits and discussions, but these would be designed for a different and longer term purpose. In summary, the communications network required should not only put like-minded people in touch with each other, but should also give those same people help and advice in developing and extending the contacts which have been made. It should be a clearing house and an advisory centre rolled into one; and, acting as a clearing house, the quality of service it would provide as an advisory centre would improve immensely. There are problems in devising the kind of organizational structure best suited to perform both functions satisfactorily. Certain facets of the work would demand large units with perhaps national coverage, whilst other facets would require smaller units operating on a regular basis with close local links. The answer seems to lie in a regional unit serving local groups of schools which has access to expensive facilities such as computing, statistical, printing and question banking services provided by a larger body serving several regions. Suggestions of this kind are being put forward at the present time (1973) in relation to a new administrative structure for a common examining system at 16+, so these ideas are not merely a mirage without substance.

The key element in the mix suggested here is the teacher who will supply most of the information. If this information is to be put to the best use, then the time at which it becomes available is almost as important as its nature. The phenomenon which can be called 'teacher modesty' is relevant here. Teachers are rarely willing to submit 'raw' plans of what they are doing, let alone tentative outlines of what they might be doing, and yet these are more important than the polished statements that they prefer to produce.

Although it seems natural to want to give a very polished statement about an idea that has been urging one to action when making it public, this line of approach has two distinct disadvantages for the development of the idea. In the first place, a statement, highly polished in the eyes of the creator, concerning an innovation in curriculum design and classroom practice, has probably been produced with much personal, lonely effort. Hence, the creator is almost bound to feel sensitive about both the statement and the idea it communicates. He or she may well resent criticism of the idea and to some extent will have frozen its immediate potential for further development through failing to work on it with others. The gap between 'raw' and 'highly polished' in terms of one's ability to expose an idea upon which one is working is subject to a large number of variables which are of no concern to us here. The important point is that a teacher's first initiative to an examining board for starting a dialogue will be more effective within the framework of that dialogue if it is written and presented early in the process of his thinking. Under these circumstances, the dialogue (even if restricted to teacher and examining board) is likely to be 'developmental' rather than almost totally 'judgemental'. This is vitally important if teachers are to feel that they really are involved in an equal partnership with an examination board and hence in the external examination system. Teachers are not easily persuaded to seek early help with a line of development they have chosen, but the position is gradually being reached in which 'tentativeness' is regarded as acceptable in our working environment. We would like to encourage teachers to take advantage of this new environment, and to make it an even more powerful ingredient in educational development through being prepared to be 'tentative' in a positive rather than in a negative way.

This phenomenon of teacher modesty has a bearing on the suggestion made earlier that examining boards should communicate 'early' statements of ideas to other interested teachers on a wide scale. As matters stand the teacher who has made a private approach to an examination board with a tentative proposal may well not give the permission needed for such dissemination. A highly polished statement from a teacher is much more likely to be given the 'publish and be damned' green light than one which is perceived as being crude. It is at this point that the examining board staff together with the existing teacher-supporting agencies (for example, inspectors, advisers, colleagues in teachers' centres) should be able to provide the encouragement necessary to make teachers feel that their ideas deserve to be aired. In this way they will not only set in motion a process which might bring them help for their own ideas, but they will also give encouragement to others who have not yet gained even a hazy understanding of their own innovatory work.

This may sound a trifle over-dramatic. The 'new idea' may be a well tried approach to educational practice of which the teacher has only recently become aware. If such is the case he can be encouraged to read about the work already done by others on this particular line of development, although this would not provide the help that association with fellow fumblers might bring. The 'new idea' may also be no more than a slight realignment of the content-matter of a traditional subject, or a relatively small variation in the way orthodox material is presented to students. These are, perhaps, both the most mundane and the most potent 'new ideas'. Tinkering with the orthodox subject syllabus and the class-teaching approach is a commonplace practice upon which much scorn has been poured by the high-priests of radical innovation, but it is the starting-place for change for many teachers, and so deserves as much attention within the communications system as other forms of 'innovation'. The 'new idea' may also take on the guise of one of a dozen well-tried techniques of teaching which contain the germ of an enquiry-based approach to learning, and they too should be viewed as 'growth points'. They deserve support and ought to be communicated to others, notwithstanding the likelihood that somewhere along the line they will be called 'old hat'. The point is that nobody is in a strong position to evaluate the growing points of others. We are all 'growing' and are thus open to the critical gaze of those who have already enjoyed the state of growth in which we find ourselves. The authors do not consider it over-dramatic to ask teachers to see themselves as humble learners who are capable of being helped by others, as well as being in a position to help even their 'helpers'! This is what education is about.

Let us make the large assumption that a position has been reached in which teachers are prepared to do two things; first to submit their ideas at an early stage to a communications network largely maintained by an examination board, and secondly to allow such submissions to be given an airing within this network. The exercise may well produce a trickle of comments from teachers who, within the supportive environment which it is hoped will have emerged, are eager to share views with a teacher who has aired his ideas in the way described. What happens next depends very much on the nature of the idea that is central to this stage of groping towards a dialogue.

The communications network can perhaps best be illustrated by seeing how it might work in a particular set of circumstances. The illustration chosen is concerned with developments in a single subject, geography. Had the choice been an integrated course or I.D.E. what follows would be equally applicable: such courses would, however, throw up one or two additional points to which attention will be drawn later.

The example concerns a teacher who is redesigning a programme in geography so that it involves fourth and fifth year students in studies and practical activities in the fields of urban geography and oceanography, with special reference to the use man makes of sea food, in addition to other, perhaps more general, studies in geography. Slightly expanded, this statement is turned into a 'declaration of intent' which is sent to an examining board, and secondly to allow such submissions to be given redesigned programme are capable of being developed and studied in ways which will draw attention to certain pressing matters of public concern, it is likely that other teachers of geography, not to mention teachers of other subjects, are thinking about their school programmes in similar ways. They may not all choose the same list of 'concerns' upon which to base their working schemes, but there may well be a measure of agreement that a geography programme, orientated towards subjects of public concern is likely to be seen as relevant by the students who will be exposed to it.

Without stretching the imagination too far, it seems reasonable to suggest that if an examining board makes known to a large number of teachers the broad outline of such a programme it will receive communications from some of those teachers who are thinking along similar lines. In such circumstances the board can call a meeting of the teachers concerned together with a member or members of its staff either at a central point or in groups in different areas. The initial 'declaration of intent' and the information supplied by other teachers who have reacted to it is made available at these meetings. This perhaps becomes the starting point for a general discussion about the potential of specialized programmes of this type in geography, and about the means of identifying the requirements to be met if such programmes are developed further and presented for assessment and certification. Thus a dialogue is started which might be followed up by various activities. For example, perhaps some teachers see that schemes of work being developed within a number of their schools are now so similar that they can form a consortium, and use a group Mode 2 or Mode 3 to mount an assessment/certification exercise. Other teachers might find that while they agreed on the broad objectives contained within an educational approach to geography to which the various 'declarations of intent' pointed, they cannot find agreement on the areas that 'should be studied'. They might be able to develop a programme similar to the one described for the World History Project, with an agreement on the title of the course and the aims of the educational work it might promote. As with the World History Project, the examining board and the teachers involved could then work towards an agreement whereby each school submits its own interpretation of the title and the aims, and then over a period of time develops an assessment pattern which involves both the teachers and the board. In fact the ideas implicit in the World History Project offer a great deal to such a programme of development in, say, 'Contemporary Geography'. Finally, there might well be teachers at the original meeting whose points of contact with the rest of the group are not sufficient for them to participate in a joint exercise. For such teachers an individual Mode 3 would constitute the best approach if they wish their course to be assessed. Some of these teachers might leave the group, while others might stay in close contact in order to obtain assistance with the development of assessment techniques. Whatever happens, there will be a considerable feedback to those who are involved with the development of Mode 1 examinations in geography within the examinations board. Moreover, in those areas of the curriculum in which geography plays a part, the development techniques used for assessing students' understanding of geographical concepts and of the skills of the geographer would benefit immensely by such a joint teacher/examining board initiative.

The stimulus for the suggestions originally put forward by the geography teacher might have been provided by the use made of materials produced as part of a curriculum development project, say one of the Schools Council projects. Much project material is produced without formal assessment and certification in mind. A study by L. A. Smith[1] has shown that many teachers have difficulties in developing appropriate assessment techniques for evaluating their success in putting over the educational activities sponsored by such material. This difficulty becomes more acute when teachers wish to have the course externally assessed and certificated. A sharing of experiences in relation to project and other materials, which can be infinitely variable, seems to be another possible use of the communications network. There is no reason at all why a storage and retrieval system for project materials and their use should not be built up as an extension to the network, and be used in association with banks of questions designed to assess the skills and concepts whose mastery and understanding the use of the materials is intended to develop. This would be particularly valuable in relation to a project like the Schools Council Humanities Project where an ounce of practical experience in the use of materials deliberately designed to stimulate discussion is worth a ton of theory. Such material and its use also create particularly acute assessment problems, and practical accounts of ways of tackling issues like the individual's contribution to a group discussion and the whole question of how to assess discussion would be invaluable. Here the communication might consist of tapes as well as of pieces of paper.

Integrated studies programmes present a peculiar problem in relation to communication. Ideas about such programmes are unique in a way which ideas about single subject programmes can never be. This results from the process of integration itself. The preparation of an integrated studies programme by a group of teachers within a school involves them in defining not only the areas of study they wish to promote but also the ways in which they see these areas interrelating. The resulting mixture of content, attitudes and concepts within the chosen subjects is bound to be unique for the group or individual who has proposed the integration. This makes it unlikely that the communication of the full programme will be of great value to other teachers, since the thinking behind it will be peculiar to the programme and not always easy to explain. The value of encouraging teachers to let others do their thinking for them in the preparation of an integrated programme is also questionable. There is no doubt, however, that contact between teachers who are engaged on differing programmes is as valuable when these are integrated as it is when they are not.

The best way to secure this contact, without in any way inhibiting freedom of action and choice, seems to lie in communicating, not the

[1] *New Resourees Dialogue,* in *Ideas* No. 27, Feb. 1974.

details, but the aims of the programmes and a list of the subjects involved. The detail may have to be provided subsequently, to the board, should the school wish to have its programmes assessed and certified. These statements of aims and lists of subjects would permit interested teachers to follow up on their own any programmes which look like potential allies. The statements of aims would also provide useful information for the board in its consideration of the assessment problems of integrated programmes, and thus in the preparation of appropriate advisory services.

Much of what was said in the preceding paragraphs about integrated programmes applies also to I.D.E. programmes. Here, however, the aims of the programmes should be supplemented not by a list of the subjects involved but by the titles of the chosen themes. Teachers with experience of I.D.E. will be able to recognize the type of enquiry-based work that is likely to be promoted by most of the themes publicized in this way. Almost certainly, while any number of themes will be put forward, they will tend to fall within a few broad categories. Thus a team of teachers in one school may well find that because of the nature of their theme they can, with profit, contact a team working in another school which has decided to work on a different or allied theme. Communications over I.D.E. programmes might thus turn out to be both easier and more fruitful over integrated programmes, although the difficulties of combining within a communications network maximum utility with the absence of any pressure to use what is provided remain formidable. It is hoped, however, that this very brief indication of some of the ways in which such a network could operate will have served to indicate its key position in the successful working of any interaction model designed to promote a freer curriculum. Perhaps its greatest value is that as it expands so do the possibilities for its further expansion, and so too does the quality of assistance that those involved can provide for each other.

In order to achieve a freer curriculum at the secondary level within the framework of externally recognized assessment and certification, this book has advocated throughout a different role for examining boards. The implementation of such a role will inevitably require different structures from those at present in existence, and will involve re-thinking the relationship that examining boards have with the rest of the education service. Ought they, for example, to continue to charge fees and make token payments to teachers, or ought they instead to be one service amongst many provided by local authorities or area training organizations for a teaching profession whose salaries are adjusted to take account of their involvement as an integral part of their professional work? Such changes will not be easy to introduce. Unless, however, a structure is found which can permit the continuous servicing of local groups of teachers and schools (with the emphasis upon the word 'local') and unless there can be found staff interested and skilled in providing consultancy services on a continuous basis, then a happy marriage between examining boards and schools will not be possible. Only through such a marriage can the potential of both curriculum development and assessment practice be properly exploited.

This changed role does not mean that the supervisory moderating function should cease to be part of the work of future examining boards. If, however, the exercise of this necessary function is not to interfere with curriculum development, then the emphasis at present placed upon comparability between boards and between subjects will have to be abandoned. Instead, moderation in the future will need to be increasingly concerned with the demands that particular curricula and the courses developed from them place upon the group who takes them. In relation to these demands, levels of performance will have to be established. If this is to be done then the first thing that must disappear is our present system of presenting results in the form of global grades. Such grades can be, and are, treated as if they represent comparable levels of performance between boards and subjects and measure in accurate fashion differences in levels of performance within subjects. Different methods of presenting information about performance will have to be introduced, and in particular profile reporting ought to be investigated in detail. If this is not done the curriculum needs of secondary schools will remain constrained by the examining system despite any efforts that examining boards may make in other directions to assist schools to develop and assess their own courses.

The book has also advocated a different role for teachers in relation to nationally recognized examinations, which many of the profession will neither consider desirable nor wish to undertake. It is also a role for which their present training in large measure does not fit them. Regrettably, considerations of space and the line of argument pursued here do not enable the authors to develop the points made in these last paragraphs in any greater detail. The willingness, however, of both examining boards and teachers to accept these changed roles is vital to the emergence of a freer curriculum at the secondary level as the authors have defined it. It is only if the willingness exists that the necessary support of other agencies within the education service such as the colleges of education and local authorities will be forthcoming. This reference, albeit brief, does, however, serve to underline once again the enormous amount of work required if we are to use the examining system in ways suggested in this book as an aid rather than as a hindrance to curriculum development. Recent developments in public examinations although encouraging have done little more than make examining boards passive partners in the developmental process, and this is not enough. The task may be long and expensive, but the rewards both for students and teachers will be enormous. It must surely be worth trying.

Proposals for the Assessment of Inter-disciplinary Enquiry (I.D.E.)

A proposal for externally examining IDE (inter-disciplinary enquiry) and integrated studies by Leslie A. Smith

The proposal in Broad Outline

1 The school will create its own programme of educational activity for its Fourth and Fifth year pupils, and will submit a detailed statement of its intentions to the Board. The statement will indicate whether or not changes in the programme are to be expected during the period of the course; and if so, the Board will stipulate the final date of amendment, say, the January of the year of examination. The school will make a reasoned statement claiming that the programme is equivalent to X number of G.C.E. certificates.

2 The Board will appoint an official who will be responsible in general terms for the school's scheme and examination. He will perform the function of an account executive as met with in advertising, and he will be the link man between school and Board. I shall call him an EXAMINATIONS CONSULTANT.

3 The Examinations Consultant will assist the school in its preparation of the initial submission, and will share the experience of designing the reasoned statement concerning equivalence of the scheme in terms of existing G.C.E. certification. He will be responsible for guiding the school's scheme through the Board's committees, and will have the power to call on school staff to assist in this direction.

4 The declaration of an AGREED EQUIVALENCE OF CERTIFICATION will be the signal for the school to proceed with its work with its Fourth year pupils firm in the knowledge that in general terms the Board will award certificates to pupils indicating that passes at G.C.E. 'O' level have been obtained in numbers contained in the range 1, 2, 3 . . . to the maximum number agreed by both school and Board.

5 The process of determining equivalence in terms of existing G.C.E. 'O' level passes is to be seen for what it is—a subjective judgment by whomsoever is involved—but attempts should be made to assist the teachers and examiners in making such judgments through the use of techniques of ITEM ANALYSIS.

6 It is essential for Inter-disciplinary Enquiry (I.D.E.) that the concept of slight

modification to the initial submission by the school is accepted as it is extremely difficult for the school working through this approach to education to forecast years in advance the full scope of the work that will be done by the pupils during the course of two years. This need for the postponement of closure is also applicable to integrated studies, although the degree to which it applies is far less crucial to the educational approach involved. Where postponement of closure is admitted, obviously, the final agreement as to equivalence of the school's submission must be postponed also; but it is to be hoped that the Board will be able to accept the submitted scheme as being 'at least equivalent to X G.C.E.s.' and then view the modifications that might be made during the ensuing years of the course as being in the nature of marginal variations to this initial decision.

7 Obviously, the Examinations Consultant working with the school will be in a strong position to guide both Board and school on these marginal variations, as he will be in close touch with both parties throughout the course.

8 The examination of the pupils will take place during the start of the summer term of the Fifth Year of secondary education. Pupils who have passed beyond this stage of their education will also, no doubt, be involved. It is not envisaged that pupils younger than those in the Fifth Year of the secondary school will take the examination.

9 The examination will be in three parts. The processes of assessment for certification purposes will be based on these three parts and in addition will include a fourth element—TEACHER ASSESSMENT.

PART ONE

10 This consists of a series of papers of appropriate length containing objective test style multiple choice questions which scan inclusively both KNOWLEDGE and HIGHER INTELLECTUAL SKILLS, and, where possible, areas of the AFFECTIVE DOMAIN (*pace* B. J. Bloom's *Taxonomies of Educational Objectives*). Viewed as a whole, this series of question papers will provide reasonable 'coverage' of the school's submitted scheme; and viewed as elements of this series, each question paper will 'cover' a PHASE of the broad area of investigation and study posed by the scheme as a whole. As far as I.D.E. is concerned, each PHASE will tend to be INTER-DISCIPLINARY, and, therefore, each question paper in the series will also tend to be inter-disciplinary. (This is an essential requirement when examining I.D.E. and the facility afforded by my proposal for Part One of the examination is one that will benefit INTEGRATED STUDIES as well although the inter-disciplinary aspect is not viewed as being of such essence in such studies.)

PART TWO

This part of the examination is a MODE THREE. It represents the POINT OF ENTRY to the total examination programme by each pupil; and for this and other reasons it is both devised and evaluated by the pupil's teachers in collaboration with the Board.

It has been designed for pupils who are engaged in I.D.E., but it is also an appropriate way of examining pupils who are undertaking integrated studies.

It necessitates the teachers in the school being aware of those aspects of the examination programme which have (*a*) provided a special attraction for each pupil, (*b*) provided a basis for a depth-study being made by any pupil and (*c*) led to a pupil making such a depth-study under guidance. Obviously, whilst it is true that any number of such special studies will be undertaken by the pupils in the school, it is likely that most of the studies made will fall into certain groups each of which will have attracted two or more pupils; and that as a consequence any test devised to examine these special studies will be at times tailor made for one pupil, and at times tailor made for a group of pupils. In I.D.E. the special studies will tend to equate with the PHASES of the broad AREA OF INVESTI-GATION that has promoted the two years' work; and, therefore, each special depth-study will tend to be inter-disciplinary. This part of the examination will take the form of a question paper to which ESSAY-STYLE responses and/or a 'MAKING' are required.

The school's Examinations Consultant will assist the teachers in compiling question papers for this part of the examination, and once made, they will be submitted to the Board which will declare that 'if a pupil takes *this* Question Paper in Part Two, he will be required to take a specified paper from the series of objective test papers that combine to create Part One of the examination'.

Thus, it is through the choice made for Part Two that the pupil is committed to appropriate sections of Part One; and this is the vehicle for both admission to the examination scheme and what can be called PRIMA FACIE CERTIFICA-TION.

Of course, a pupil might submit himself (or be submitted by the school if this view is more acceptable) to one paper in Part Two, or any number of such papers; each representing a depth-study of a phase (or conjoint phases) or an otherwise examination-appropriate area of study. Where two such entries are made in Part Two, two appropriate sections of Part One will be deemed by the Board to be necessary to the pupil's examination; and so on until the pupil's entries in Part Two are such that he will be required to take the complete series of tests devised for Part One. Such a candidate would be submitting himself for examina-tion in the number of G.C.E.s. agreed by both Board and school as being appro-priate to the work that the school's scheme involves.

PART THREE

This part of the examination involves an appraisal of the pupil's ability to cope with the PROCESSES of ENQUIRY, MAKING and DIALOGUE. It is a largely untried area of examination technique, and as such it should be seen as an EXPERIMENTAL part of my proposals.

I would like to see each pupil who enters the examination being given the opportunity of demonstrating how he can cope with the processes of learning mentioned. This is of vital concern to the approach to education represented by I.D.E., and as these processes are key operational objectives within this ap-proach it seems reasonable to state that the coping powers of the pupils in these basic human activities should be considered in terminal examinations as well as throughout the course.

For a start, I envisage the appraisal taking the form of observation and assessment of a pupil's performance when, in response to a broadly based question he has been posed, he prepares a PLAN OF CAMPAIGN which will indicate that he is able to:

(*a*) understand the question posed;
(*b*) use the resources provided to familiarize himself with the knowledge required to propose an answer to it;
(*c*) prepare a statement consisting of a flow of questions or statements which illustrates his logic, his approach to the key problem, his resourcefulness in presenting his argument;
(*d*) prepare a series of statements which illustrate how he will express points of his argument to his audience and so demonstrate his powers of communication and creative flow.

In many respects, I see this 'plan of campaign' as being similar to an author's outline as he prepares to research and write and illustrate a book on a subject of personal concern. Undoubtedly, there are many other ways of appraising these processes of enquiry, making, and dialogue, and I hold no brief for the one I have proposed except to say that I have used it for sixteen years internally in schools with some effect.

I would suggest that Part Three of the proposed examination scheme be viewed as an experimental area for the initial stages of any examination programme that might emerge from my proposals being accepted and used; and during this period, whilst candidates would take Part Three tests, the appraisal would take a 'satisfactory'/'not satisfactory' form.

Later, perhaps, as experience is gained, I would expect to see this part of the examination programme given the status that it deserves, *viz.*, a part in which a successful assessment must be obtained by a candidate if he is to be considered for certification at 'O' level. But in view of the fact that such an element is absent from existing G.C.E. examinations at 'O' level, it would be unfair to write into a new scheme a requirement which is both experimental in nature and additional to current examination requirements.

During the experimental nature of this part of the examination, I suggest that it be conducted under Mode 1 with a developmental programme instituted to turn it into a Mode 2 and then a Mode 3 examination appraisal. Obviously, this is an area for the school's Examination Consultant to work in.

11 The three parts of the examination would provide for each of the school's candidates a PRIMA FACIE CERTIFICATION. Performance on the Part One tests would be judged by the Board; and the school would deal with the Part Two tests. Initially, as suggested, the Board would assess the pupil's performance in Part Three with, perhaps, each pupil being given the opportunity of choosing his 'best performances' from a series of such situation-style tests.

12 Thus, the results of Part One, Two and Three of the examination for a candidate might look like the table shown overleaf.

Therefore, Prima Facie Certification in this example would be two G.C.E. passes at grades 5 and 3.

		Results		
		A	B	C
Part One	Three papers, A, B & C, related to Part Two studies	27%	24%	32%
Part Two	Three studies made by candidate, A, B & C, each assessed through a special examination	28%	20%	35%
	Combined score for Parts One & Two	55%	44%	67%
	Assessment Grades awarded for Parts One & Two	5	7	3
		a sat.	b unsat.	c sat.
Part Three	Three tests taken and assessed as being 'satisfactory' or 'unsatisfactory'			

13 At this point, I propose to introduce the concept of the TEACHERS ASSESSMENT so that a final examination result can be obtained.

The pupil's work during the two year period of the course will be subject to continual (if not continuous) appraisal (both self-appraisal and teacher-appraisal). This will be the type of appraisal that leads to ACTION on behalf of the pupil and not assessment for the sake of records only. As such it will lead to a high degree of relevance to the pupil's educational development and could well become locally in each school a relatively efficient process.

I would hope to see a great deal of experimenting taking place to ascertain the ingredients of any such appraisal programme, and certainly I would expect to see the school's Examination Consultant heavily involved with his colleagues in both Board and schools helping to develop suitable appraisal check-lists and appraisal techniques whilst accepting the role within his consultative function as a person who is able to guide teachers in the processes of appraisal that are found to be desirable from the points of view of examination and certification.

A statement will be prepared by the school for each pupil entering the examination either during the month before the examination or (as I prefer) on two occasions, i.e. October and April of the Fifth Year of the school course. (I consider the two statements as being desirable because they would present a range for each area of behaviours being appraised which MIGHT be representative of an earlier pessimistic view and a later optimistic view of the candidate's likely performance at the Spring external examination).

Concluding the statement(s) from the school will be a forecast as to the number of G.C.E. certificates each candidate is expected to obtain as a result of the work he has done and the examinations he will take (and possibly some forecast as to grades).

Thus, the Board will have an examination result for each candidate based upon the Parts One, Two and Three of the examination programme; and it will also be in possession of a reasoned forecast from the school of the result to be expected which is itself supported either by one or two statements of appraisals made during the period leading up to the examination.

If the results obtained by the examination agree with the forecast made by the school, then the candidate will be awarded the certificates in the grades concerned without further enquiry.

If the candidates' results obtained by the examination are greater than the results forecast by the school, then I suggest that the examination results should stand and the appropriate certificates and grades awarded.

If, on the other hand, the candidate's results obtained by the examination are less than those forecast by the school, an enquiry will take place. This enquiry will be dealt with in the first instance by the school's Examinations Consultant and the staff of the school involved; and this officer may well find it necessary to bring in other experts.

The Examinations Consultant and his co-opted consultants will act as MODER-ATORS who will seek to resolve the differences between the school's forecasts and the examination results.

How this process is executed is a matter for experiment and development, but the principle I am putting forward is one which will involve the Board granting the award of certification to the candidates concerned on the basis of the agreements reached between moderators and school staff.

To facilitate this part of the programme, I suggest that the external examinations should take place as early as possible in the Summer Term (possibly May) and that the marking and declaration of examination results should be dealt with most expeditiously (possibly mid-June). Not every candidate's work and records will have to be moderated, of course, but it will be necessary for a sample of the work and records of those who are not subject to moderation to be viewed by the moderators, so that they may be better briefed to perform their function for the candidates who are declared to be subject to moderation. This work will take time; and it is best done, in my opinion, when the pupils concerned are still members of the school's population. Hence the urgency in arriving at the prima facie certification.

L. A. S.
March 1968

Inter-disciplinary enquiry by Henry G. Macintosh

The examination of I.D.E. presents problems, since assessment inevitably demands definition in order that decisions are taken upon what is or is not to be examined. It is not necessary for this definition to have a restrictive effect, although this may result if the area selected for assessment is a narrow one. The problem is aggra-vated in the present situation as regards secondary school examining in this coun-try. The G.C.E. and the C.S.E. are, in the main, single subject examinations, and success is recorded upon the certificate by means of single lines describing the subjects. Such a certification runs contrary to the whole ethos of I.D.E. which aims at breaking down the barriers between subjects. It is, however, inescapable at the present time, and any external examination must in some sense remain a compromise between the requirement of the schools, who will be organising flexible work in inter-disciplinary enquiry with different pupils undertaking different work, and the need for the examining board to have some subject matter which they can classify for the purpose of certification.

The scheme proposed below should be seen in this light, although it is worth making the point that some definition, implying as it does a statement of objectives, will provide a framework which may help the school and avoid the possibility of work being undertaken in a wholly undisciplined fashion.

The remainder of this paper is concerned with the outline of the proposed examination and suggestions as to how it would be operated in practice. Before doing this, however, it is essential to make one further general point: that there must be a separate examination for each school, since no two schools will make the same decision in relation to I.D.E. The outline which follows is, therefore, nothing more than a guide, and if there are fifty schools being examined then there will almost certainly be fifty different ways in which the outline will be filled in. The four components of the proposed examination are as follows:

1 test of basic skills
2 tests of subject abilities and skills
3 project work
4 continuous assessment

As far as the Board is concerned the first step would be a request from a school to examine their I.D.E. programme. Upon receipt of such a request the Board would require the school to provide it with the following information:

(i) the amount of time that they are devoting to I.D.E.
(ii) the number of lines of G.C.E. certification they would regard their proposals as being equivalent to, e.g., one, two, three or four subjects with no attempt at defining subjects
(iii) the subject areas which I.D.E. is replacing and the general areas of study in which they think that the pupils will be involved during the programme.

The purpose of the first and second points is, I think, obvious, but the third may perhaps raise doubts since it has the appearance of trying to draw lines before the course has even started. Such information is, however, essential if any realistic dialogue is to take place between the Board and the school in Parts I, ll and II of the scheme. A practical illustration may perhaps clarify the issue. A school states that it will be devoting the equivalent of seventeen periods a week to I.D.E.; that this will cover time which had previously been occupied with English, history, geography and religious knowledge, and that it would regard the following additional areas as being ones in which their pupils were likely to undertake work: sociology, economics, civics, art, history and pottery. Before the next stage can be undertaken the Board will have to decide whether or not it is prepared to accept that the general proposal is worth X subjects as far as certification is concerned. Unless the school has this assurance it cannot possibly be asked to embark on the extensive work which the subsequent stages will involve.

Basic Skills

We will assume therefore, that in the case of the school mentioned the Board has agreed to an equivalence of four subjects. The Board will then ask the school to set down the basic skills which it considers candidates ought to acquire as a result of taking the course and which they would like to see assessed. What is included in this list of basic skills will be in part a reflection of what subjects the I.D.E. programme is replacing; e.g. if English is still being taught outside I.D.e. then the school may well not wish to have verbal fluency tested as a basic skill, whereas if English is within the I.D.E. programme it is more than likely that they will wish to see it included. Such basic skills as reading comprehension, ability to plan individual work, ability to analyse written material and to determine the relevance of material, might be included. It is emphasized that it is for the school to decide what basic skills are to be tested and for the examining board to decide whether and how these are to be tested by means of an external examination. Such decisions can only be reached if the school rigorously defines its objectives. The basic skills test which results will be attempted by all candidates taking the programme, probably at the end of the second term of the fifth year. The objectives and the skills to be assessed in the test will be known to all the pupils.

Subject Abilities and Skills

In its initial proposal the school will have indicated the number of subject areas in which they consider pupils involved in the I.D.E. programme will undertake work, although it will not say in which areas any particular pupil will be working. This list may contain as many as ten or twelve subject areas and will be decided by the school. For the Board the list will represent the subjects in which it is willing to provide examinations in subject skills. Note that the words used are 'subject abilities and skills': the examination in history will not be a test of knowledge of content, it will be a test of general historical understanding. Just as it has defined the basic skills, the school will be asked to define what it considers pupils ought to be able to do, or, in other words, what abilities they ought to be able to demonstrate in each of the subject areas. The choice as to which particular areas they are to be assessed upon will be left to the pupils under guidance from the school. This decision, it is suggested, should be taken by the pupils at the end of the first term of the fourth year. Pupil X, for example, may choose to be assessed in history, sociology, English and pottery; Pupil Y in English, geography, economics and art history. Each pupil will make a different choice and it is this choice of subjects that will be recorded on the certificate if they are successful in them. Upon making their choice they will be informed of the abilities upon which they will be tested in each area. It is essential, therefore, that the school ensures that pupils make choices appropriate to their subsequent career requirements: e.g. if English is included in an I.D.E. programme, it is clear that under present circumstances all pupils would need to choose to be assessed in English. When the choice has been made it is presumed that the pupils will thereafter direct their attention more specifically to their chosen areas than to other areas. While this imposes some slight restriction, it is believed that this will not be burdensome and may indeed provide valuable definition, more particularly as the pupils will not be assessed on content knowledge.

Projects

It is assumed that after making their choice of subjects pupils will undertake project work in these areas, and that this will result in sufficient work being available for assessment which can be identified as falling broadly into a particular compartment for assessment purposes. This limitation will also have the practical effect of ensuring that the majority of the work to be assessed will not be undertaken before the second term of the fourth year, which is almost certainly desirable. Assessment of this work will be carried out by the school, subject to moderation by the Board, and a decision will need to be taken on the minimum number of projects required for each subject area, probably two, making eight pieces of work in all.

Continuous Assessment

This element in the assessment will be produced by the school and will not be subject to moderation by the Board. It is assumed that the school will keep a complete record of the work undertaken by all pupils. Indeed there is a good case for the Board requesting such a record in the unlikely event of the school not maintaining it. This will include all activities which the pupils have undertaken and will indicate their industry, their approach to the work, their improvement, and so on. The school will be required to make subjective decisions upon this record and convert it to a mark which will form a component of the final assessment.

To summarize, therefore, the four elements of the examination will be as follows:

1 A basic skills test set by the Board on the basis of objectives supplied by the school and discussed and agreed with the Board. Although only one score will result from this test it will be applied to each of the subjects in which the candidate is being examined in Part II.

2 A number of tests of subject skills set by the Board on the basis of objectives defined by the school and discussed and agreed with the Board. Each pupil will take whatever number of tests the school's I.D.E. programme has been deemed to be equivalent to, but they will have a choice within the area of original agreement.

3 Project work for each area in which tests of subject skills are taken. This will be assessed by the school but subject to moderation by the Board.

4 Continuous assessment by the school based on the child's overall performance on the course as a whole. This should avoid being based solely on particular pieces of work and should consist rather of a 'global impression' of the candidates and their work.

Mark Weighting of the Components

This is extremely difficult and can be decided in a variety of ways according to the criteria adopted. For example: (i) should the Board aim at providing the majority of marks on tests set by itself, or should the majority of the marks come from the school? (ii) Should the Board insist on the majority of marks being awarded to work which can be identified as belonging exclusively to particular subjects, or should the majority go to general work which cannot be so readily compartmentalized? To state criteria in this rather stark form does less than justice to the compromises which, as suggested in the opening paragraph, have inevitably to be built into the whole scheme, but such criteria have nevertheless to be borne in mind. The mark weighting given below (out of 100 for convenience) is essentially a tentative one but is intended to effect a balance which it is considered is appropriate to the whole course.

1 Basic Skills Test	20/100
2 Subject Abilities and Skills Test	40/100
3 Projects	25/100
4 Continuous Assessment	15/100

The marks gained in 2 and 4 would apply to all subjects, so that if a pupil gained 15/100 in Part 1 and 8/100 in Part 2, he would carry over 23/100 to each of his subjects. The marks in 2 and 3 would vary with each subject.

H. G. M.
July 1968

Associated Examining Board Pilot Project in the Assessment of World History at 'O' Level

For the past eighteen months a special working party of the A.E.B. has been meeting to consider new methods of assessment in World History at Ordinary Level. As a result, a new approach to the assessment of history has been devised which the Board aims to try out in the form of a pilot project over the next two years, 1971 and 1972. World History was chosen for the pilot project for three main reasons. First, an understanding of twentieth century World History is important because, in an increasingly interdependent world, it gives the background and perspective necessary for an understanding of current problems from a global rather than from a national or continental view. Secondly, it was chosen because there is ample evidence of its increasing popularity in both schools and colleges of further education. Thirdly, it lends itself particularly well to a study of an essentially inter-disciplinary nature.

The assessment will be based upon an offer to centres of (a) the title, (b) the aims of the course, (c) the structure of the assessment.

Title

'History of World Powers and World Events in the 20th Century'

Aims

The aims of the course upon which the assessment will be based are:

(a) to foster an understanding of the significance of change and continuity for for historical study;

(b) to promote an awareness of the availability of primary and secondary sources;

(c) to encourage the use and evaluation of materials of various types;

(d) to elicit from the student imaginative and empathetic responses;

(e) to encourage students to communicate their personal understanding and involvement through historical study.

Structure

The scheme to assess the above aims will be a mixture of Mode 1 and Mode 3. In addition to a written paper, which will be sent by the Board but based upon the teaching programmes submitted by the participating centres, there will be a project in which oral work will play an important part. The choice of the project topic will be made by the centre, subject to approval by the Board, and will be assessed initially by the centre and subsequently moderated by the Board. The assessment in the written paper will consist of questions ranging in a spectrum from completely open-ended essay questions to completely closed objective questions. In the assessment of the project the Board is concerned with three aspects: (i) plans of campaign, (ii) execution, (iii) use of resources. To provide further guidance to schools considering taking up the offer, a detailed explanation of the title, aims and structure follows.

1 The Title

The title of the course to be assessed is 'History of World Powers and World Events in the 20th Century'. It is intended by the Board that the work undertaken should consist of a study of world powers and of events which, while not necessarily involving world powers, are nevertheless of concern to them.

2 The Aims

The Board would wish to make the following points by way of a gloss upon these aims.

(a) To foster the understanding of the significance of change and continuity for historical study

The understanding of change and continuity in history is theoretically an extremely complex one but it is considered to be central to any historical study in its practical applications. For example, a study of the rise of Hitler and the Nazi Party in Germany would be a limited one if, on the one hand, it took no account of the possible existence of certain recurring themes in German history or gave no consideration to the problem of national characteristics; or, on the other, if it failed to recognize the effects of the First World War upon Germany and Europe. In the assessment this first aim has general application, that is to say, those taking the assessment will be given credit in all work submitted for their understanding of the problem in relation to particular countries and particular events.

(b) To promote an awareness of the availability of primary and secondary sources

(c) To encourage the use and evaluation of sources of various types

These two aims run into one another in the sense that awareness of the existence of resource materials of all kinds is essential before their use in historical study, and before the making of judgments about their value in relation to any particular piece of work being undertaken. It is suggested that there are four distinct stages contained within these two aims.

(i) To acquaint students in general terms with the extent and availability of resource material.

(ii) To enable students to understand in general terms the strengths and weaknesses, the advantages and disadvantages, of different types of resource material, including textbooks, and to provide them with guide lines for the handling of material in the light of these considerations.

(iii) To show students how to establish criteria for the finding, selecting and organizing of material in relation to specific problems or areas of study.

(iv) To encourage students to examine critically all resource material which they use in terms of its appropriateness, relevance and reliability to the problem under consideration. This will bring students to the realization that the availability and reliability of resource material may compel alterations in the approach to the study of any particular problem, and may on occasion require a re-statement of the problem itself.

In the context of this course, the Board does not wish too rigid an interpretation to be placed upon the word 'primary' in connection with resource material. It would accept as a primary source any source of relevant information apart from a standard history book and it would hope that those teaching the course would take advantage of circumstances to encourage the use of all kinds of materials, some of which might not be 'primary' in the strict interpretation of the word.

Aims (*b*) and (*c*) will be assessed both in the project and in the written part of the assessment, the project being particularly appropriate for this purpose. Specific questions may be set involving resource materials and at all times students will be given credit for reference to resources when these are relevant and appropriate.

(d) To elicit from the student imaginative and empatheic responses

The aim here is to encourage students to develop a feeling for the past. One is not concerned here primarily with the judgment of history upon actions in the light of subsequent knowledge, but with a re-creation of the past in order to try and show the reasons and motives for action. This is not a simple task and can all too easily degenerate into an artificial exercise of the 'imagine you are a Red Guard' kind. If it is to be well done it will involve a close study of resource material and the involvement of disciplines other than history. It will be as much concerned with ideas, ideologies, hypotheses and theories as with facts.

(e) To encourage pupils to communicate their personal understanding and involvement through historical study.

The vital words here are 'understanding', 'involvement' and 'communicate'. In order to understand something the pupil needs to know it and to know it accurately and in detail. Knowledge is thus a key to understanding and not something of value in itself. Real understanding of a problem, of a chain of events or of a personality, permits students to become personally involved in a way which is not possible when something is partly known and half understood. Finally, communication is the means by which this understanding and involvement is conveyed to others either on paper or by word of mouth. Unless this is done properly then much of what has gone before will be lost. This aim, like the first, will have universal application.

3 *Weighting of the Aims and Assessment of the Course*

No attempt has been made to weight the aims specifically in relation to each other As has already been stated, Aims (*a*) and (*e*) will have universal application. Of the other three, Aims (*b*) and (*c*) will be specifically catered for in the project and (*d*) in the written paper, possibly by means of a compulsory question, additional credit being given elsewhere as and when it is considered appropriate and the questions asked permit or require it. If a compulsory question is used, then all the information necessary to answer the question will be provided in the question itself.

(*a*) *The written part*
In the written part of the assessment the aims will be assessed by means of a wide range of question types and it is anticipated that a large number of the questions asked will consist of several parts, some of which may be open-ended and some closed, so that within questions as well as between questions there will be a range of different approaches to questioning.

(*b*) *The project*
In the assessment of the project, upon which it is envisaged the student will work for some three to four months, the Board is concerned with (i) the plan of campaign, (ii) the execution with particular reference to intensity of treatment, (iii) use of resources.

These three aspects will be given the following mark weighting:

(i) 11/35 (written 8, oral 3).
(ii) 12/35 (written 8, oral 4).
(iii) 12/35 (written 8, oral 4).

From the above it will be seen that a great deal of importance is attached to the oral assessment which at each stage will be conducted by the teacher acting in his dual role of supervisor and assessor. A moderator, appointed by the Board, may at any stage of the project conduct an oral assessment.

It is hoped that throughout the course there will be a series of studies in depth and not merely a single terminal project. Indeed it would be possible to build the whole course around such a series, with the students working at times altogether, at other times in small groups, and at other times again on their own. In this situation the teacher would provide the links necessary to ensure that a broad total framework was presented. Within this framework the depth studies would serve both as highlights and as the medium of communication through which the course advanced.

The Plan of Campaign

The Board would envisage the plan of campaign as containing three broad sections.

1 A list of statements and questions which the student has devised for his chosen topic. This will reveal, both as single items and in their sequence, the nature of the argument that the student will subsequently develop as he executes the plan.
2 Notes and references to resources and activities related to the statements and questions in 1 which the student sees as being relevant to his enquiries and to a proper communication of his ideas.
3 An outline of the way in which the student plans to reveal his understanding of his subject to a wider audience and to communicate his findings.

In addition to the original plan of campaign submitted with the title, which will remain unaltered as part of the evidence to be assessed, students should submit modifications of the plan, where appropriate, in order to take account of difficulties encountered as the work progresses. The number of such modifications is not limited, and the final submission might thus include the project itself, the original plan of campaign, two modified versions and the version finally used.

One of the main purposes of the oral assessment of this part of the project is to ascertain to what extent the student has had to modify his original proposals and why. The oral assessment will thus be continuous and reveal at all stages the student's campaign strategy and his understanding of the problems he encounters. Assessment would involve a discussion of how the student planned his research, the need for modification of his plan at various stages, how the work had been presented, and the reason why it had been relatively successful or unsuccessful. The Board is as much concerned, therefore, with the emergence of the plan in relation to the question 'does it work' as it is with the polished final version.

In addition to the plan of campaign for the project itself, each student will be asked to produce plans of campaign for at least two other studies in depth undertaken during terms two to five of the two year course. These can either be plans for a study actually undertaken but without the study itself, or plans for a study which was never undertaken.

The Execution

The Board's main concern with the execution of the plan lies in the 'intensity of treatment' and here we would like to draw attention to the notion of 'thresholds'. Consideration of the teaching of the course might suggest to the teacher a number of major topics or themes to form the basis of the course or a part of the course, such as Migration, Revolutionary Movements, Sovereignty/Independence, Communications and Transport, World Trade, Technological

Developments, Alliances, World Organizations and Ideologies. These would be regarded by the Board as first threshold topics. One possible breakdown of the topic 'Ideologies' is provided below, but it is stressed that many possible topics could be chosen and those chosen could be broken down in many different ways.

Ideologies: 1 Fascism in Italy, Spain, France, USA.
2 The rise of the Nazi party in Germany.
3 The Marxist doctrine and the West: the growth of socialist parties.
4 The Communist bloc: modifications in doctrine, divisions and difficulties.

These the Board would regard as second threshold topics which can in their turn be broken down into smaller and more specific topics which it would call third threshold topics, the variety of which is almost endless. In general the Board would suggest that the teacher or teachers taking the course should be teaching to second threshold topics and that projects should develop from third threshold topics. Looked at in another way, it could be said that second threshold topics lend themselves to assessment more appropriately through essays. Indeed a student in starting upon a project might well deal with the preliminaries, which are likely to be at the second threshold level, by means of an introductory essay.

This idea of thresholds will not always work out so neatly in practice. For example, biographical treatment of the great figures of the twentieth century can in the main be regarded as being at the second threshold level; on the other hand a particular course might be taught largely through the lives of certain key figures of the twentieth century and, in consequence, the intensity of treatment would go beyond this level. In such circumstances it would be a matter of debate whether a project based on a biographical study ought to treat the individual's career as a whole or to pick up particular aspects of it for more detailed treatment.

Use of Resources

As far as the use of resources is concerned, this has already been covered in the explanation provided in relation to Aims (*b*) and (*c*). Again the Board would like to stress that, in its opinion, the key question is, 'Will it work?' To answer this question satisfactorily the candidate must enquire, apply appropriate criteria, select or reject, and organize; functions which seem to be the essence of any enquiry-based study in depth.

Procedure for Registering a Project

The following procedure for registering a project with the Board will be adopted. Not earlier than 1 June and not later than 24 October in the year prior to the taking of the written assessment, all students in the participating centres will submit, through the centre, a project title together with a detailed outline of how they propose to carry out the project (the plan of campaign). This will be approved or rejected by the Board within three weeks of receipt and if rejected the student will be required to make a re-submission. Projects which will be the work of more than one student can be submitted, but in such cases the individual contribution of each student must be clearly stated and worked out. More than one student from the same school can submit the same project title provided the treatment is different. In exceptional circumstances a final project title may be agreed as late as 1 February of the year in which the written assessment takes place. This proviso is designed to assist students who, having embarked upon an agreed project, find that unexpected difficulties arise or that an alternative idea proves more rewarding. All projects must be completed by 1 May, together with the plans of campaign for the two other studies in depth, the titles of which will be chosen by the students themselves. They will be assessed in the first place by the centre in accordance with criteria laid down by the Board. This initial assessment will include a taped oral with the student upon each project and the assessment will then be moderated by the Board.

Arrangements for the Pilot Scheme

No attempt has been made in this paper to prescribe the method of teaching the course or of laying down the content, although a number of suggestions about possible approaches to teaching have been made. In order to ensure, however, that the written part of the assessment provides a proper opportunity for all students taking it, teachers in centres who wish to take part in the pilot scheme are required to send to the Board, by 22 October 1970, an outline of how they propose to teach the course, together with an indication of the content they expect to cover. The submission of such an outline is regarded by the Board as an integral part of participation in the pilot scheme and should be as detailed as the teacher is prepared to make it. The Board will use these outlines to help it in the preparation of the questions for try-out by the participating centres at the end of the first year of the course, and in the preparation of the final assessment. By so doing, the Board believes that it can provide the necessary flexibility in the assessment without in any way restricting the school's freedom of choice. It must, however, be stressed that, whatever the content, the assessment will be based upon the five stated aims and the questions asked will be designed to measure the students' ability to achieve these aims.

September 1970

Possible Models of Assessment Techniques for use within the World History Project

A working paper prepared by Leslie A. Smith

This is a working paper. It attempts to suggest ways in which the five aims devised by the Working Party may be assessed, but I wish to stress that it is not a model of a 'typical examination' but rather an attempt to produce a spectrum of assessment techniques for the written part of any test that may be used during and at the end of a two year course leading to G.C.E. certification. The paper also contains suggestions as to the way in which the 'project' element of the assessment procedure might be dealt with. This will be considered both in relation to our study of the processes employed by any student and to the ways in which he has used his studies-in-depth to help him gain an understanding of the history of world powers and world events in the twentieth century. This last will involve the use of an oral interview. It is hoped that this paper, although tentative in every respect, will have some use within the development of the assessment side of the Project. It may well also possess transfer-potential within the framework of techniques used for the assessment of single subjects, integrated studies and inter-disciplinary enquiry.

This working paper is in two parts: (1) contains a series of questioning techniques designed to probe a student's performance within the compass of the five aims chosen by the working party; (2) provides an analysis of the nature of the 'project' or study-in-depth which will be a constant feature of the work done by a student throughout the 'course' and, one would hope, throughout the period of secondary schooling. An approach is also suggested for the development of this side of the student's studies and for its assessment. In Part 1, reference is made to the five aims that are involved by the display of numbers each of which refers to one of these aims. It is helpful, therefore, to repeat these aims in the numerical sequence to which reference will be made throughout the working-paper.

The aims of the History Project

1 To foster an understanding of the significance of change and continuity for historical study.
2 To promote an awareness of the availability of primary and secondary sources.
3 To encourage the use and evaluation of materials of various types.
4 To elicit from the student imaginative and empathetic responses.

5 To encourage students to communicate their personal understanding and involvement through historical study.

I would like to add that the questions I have devised are very much of the order
of 'first drafts'. They have not been subjected to the normal processes of discussion
and editing.

Examples of Questions for the Proposed Written Examination

Question 1

The passport of a British Citizen contains the following statement: 'Her Britannic
Majesty's Principal Secretary of State for Foreign Affairs Requests and requires in
the Name of Her Majesty all those whom it may concern to allow the bearer to
pass freely without let or hindrance, and to afford the bearer such assistance and
protection as may be necessary.

Let us imagine that on three separate occasions, in the years 1910, 1942 and 1968,
British Citizens had been 'wrongfully detained' by local officials in China.

Bearing in mind the statement contained in the passport of a British Citizen,
develop an argument which supports your views as to the action that might have
been taken on behalf of these 'detainees' by the British Government firstly in the
year 1910, secondly in 1942, and thirdly in 1968.

NOTES ON QUESTION I
This question is aimed mainly at Objective 4 (eliciting imaginative and empathetic
responses) and would promote a full essay response. It also involves Objectives 1 and
5, and would reveal an understanding of the processes of comparison, trend-develop-
ment and interpretation, and 'patch' study. I accept that it is a difficult question,
but I have tried to get away from 'imagine that you are Hitler...' type of question.

NOTES ON 'TRIGGERS' FOR THIS TYPE OF QUESTION
I think that I have found a useful trigger for this type of question. It concerns the
concept of 'the jump' in reasoning. For example, if a photograph of idle mills
in Lancashire is shown purporting to be taken in 1931 and another photograph
taken in 1948 showing idle mills in Lancashire is also presented, does it follow
that such a view presents a true 'picture' of the mills of Lancashire throughout
the period 1932–48? The mental jump that is made in response to the information
provided might be highly imaginative!

Question 2

There are five parts to this question.

Briefly describe the situations that gave rise to the following statements made
by Sir Winston Churchill, War-time Prime Minister of Britain:

(*a*) 'Never in the field of human conflict was so much owed by so many to
so few.' (Broadcast speech, 1940)

(*b*) 'It may almost be said "Before Alamein we never had a victory. After
Alamein we never had a defeat." ' (History of The Second World War)

(c) 'No one has been a more consistent opponent of Communism than I have for the last twenty-five years. I will unsay no word I have spoken about it. But all this fades away before the spectacle which is now unfolding. The past, with its crimes, its follies, and its tragedies flashes away . . . we shall give whatever help we can to Russia and the Russian people.' (Broadcast, 1941)

(d) 'We shall fight on the beaches, in the fields and in the streets . . . We shall never surrender.' (Broadcast, 1940)

(e) On the subject of the Battle of Midway, 1942: 'At one stroke the dominant position of Japan in the Pacific was reversed.' (History of the Second World War)

NOTES ON QUESTION 2

The sub-division of the question into parts is to achieve a wide range of questions and to indicate to the pupil that paragraphing rather that a straight-forward essay is called for. It will take about 20/30 minutes to answer, however, and might be reduced in size. This type of question, however, puts the pupil in contact with historical commentary whilst providing a good deal of information in the question. It can be used alongside original documents, or recorded and accepted facts about events, or both; and the questions would then be couched in terms which sought a comparison and evaluation of statements and perceptions AND events.

I think that the questions I have presented spans all but the resources objectives; and with the addition of resources could cover all of them.

Question 3

Why was 1947 the year in which the creation of the new States of Pakistan and India HAD to take place?

NOTES ON QUESTION 3

This is a question requiring an essay-style response. It has the virtue of drawing upon the pupil's associated knowledge and general understanding of a multitude of facets of the situation in India not only in 1947 but before, during and after this year. It is an INTER-DISCIPLINARY question, and involves all objectives other than those dealing with resources. If possible, it would be useful if press-cuttings and photographs could be provided for the pupil, but this is not an essential part of the question. Of course, the question swings round the word HAD; and would be assessed according to the way the pupil understood what was expected of him.

I think that this is a most useful technique for promoting questions of both essay and 'short-answer' types. Its uses are limitless; and it reveals a different approach to eliciting the pupil's knowledge and understanding HISTORICALLY speaking.

Question 4

There are three parts to this question. Write briefly about each part spending about ten minutes on each.

The States of India and Pakistan were created on the 15th August, 1947.

(*a*) Why was the partition of the Indian sub-continent viewed as being the only solution to the problems of this region of the world at that time?

(*b*) What is the problem that concerns the area known as Kashmir?

(*c*) How was the problem of the Princely Sates resolved in the process of partition of this region?

NOTES ON QUESTION 4

This format is one form of alternative to Question 3; it is more orthodox. Like most questions requiring short answers it seeks knowledge and some evaluation of the situation. It is more specific than Question 3, but in many ways not so interesting. It would be helped by the provision of The India Act, 1947, or extracts from it; and also by press cuttings of the time.

Question 5

There are two parts to this question.

(*a*) Draw up a list of *ten* key-questions that you would ask yourself if you were mounting a study of the development of aircraft and their uses during the period 1914 to 1970. Place these questions in a sequence so that they show how you would present your study in written form.

(*b*) Draw up a list of the *sources* you would expect to use in the course of your enquiry into aircraft development.

NOTES ON QUESTION 5

This question represents an attempt to use the technique of the 'Plan of Campaign' which is a feature of the Personal Topic. It is aimed at objectives 1, 2, 3 and 5.

The technique lends itself to topics which are reasonably familiar territory to the pupils: it would need a great deal of preparation to use it for a topic like 'The Russian Revolution'. I feel that it is an important way of revealing the processes of studying and presenting history; and in particular it gains from being of the 'line of development' model of historical analysis.

Another format for part (*a*) could be the provision of a ten-box grid with the requirement that the pupil fills in the squares with statements and/or questions which reveal how he would approach the study.

Yet another way is to ask the pupil to make such a grid with the further requirement that he then writes questions to be answered in the style of an examiner. This might be very revealing.

I would expect questions of this type to require at least 15 minutes to answer, and maybe it will be found that they equate to essays in the time required. The advantage that this type of question has over the essay lies in the requirement that the pupil ASKS himself questions: a key-objective of a true enquiry process.

Question 6

Using the copy of the Constitution of the United Nations provided, answer the following questions:

(*a*) Which countries are permanent members of the Security Council?

(*b*) How are the other members of the Security Council elected, and for how long does each sit on the Council for any one spell?

(*c*) What part does the 'veto' play in the deliberations of the Security Council?

(*d*) Can the veto be overruled by the General Assembly? If so, how is this done?

(*e*) How is a new member admitted to the United Nations?

(*f*) What checks are applied to the decision-making powers of the Secretary General?

(*g*) How are the activities of the United Nations financed?

NOTES ON QUESTION 6

This question is aimed at objectives 2 and 3 particularly. The provision of the 'primary resource', in this case the constitution of the U.N., is an essential part of it; and it may be appropriate to provide such material some weeks before the examination takes place so that the pupil can study it in advance, and bring it to the examination room with him. I feel that this technique will encourage the testing of the objectives mentioned under examination-conditions, and will not encourage the examiners to attempt to achieve the evaluation of these objectives through the provision of snippets of information QUOTED from the original documents concerned. Obviously, this technique has wide scope. It can be used for testing the processes of 'comparison' in historical terms, for example. I have worked on a small set of constitutions (The U.N., the T.U.C. and the T.G.W.U.) —a copy of each would be supplied to the pupil in advance of the test— so that the principles of 'constitutions' can be perceived and this perception evaluated in examination-terms. This is not necessarily appropriate to the examination we are considering here, but it is a useful technique which might find a use in World History, e.g. in the principles underlying 'treaties' or 'peace settlements' or 'trade agreements' (like E.E.C. compared with E.F.T.A.).

Question 7

The grid displays six facets of American History during the years 1917/41.

Declaration of war against Germany, 1917	Refusal to join the League of Nations	Investment of capital in South America (Pan-americanism)
Aid given to Britain through Lend-Lease Act, 1941	Wall Street Stock-Market Crash triggers World Slump, 1929	Declaration of war against Axis Powers, 1941

In an essay, describe your opinion of the attitudes of the government and people of the United States at the time of each of these events in relation to their attitude concerning the policy that is called 'Isolationism'.

NOTES ON QUESTION 7

This is an extremely difficult question. It is probably too hard for G.C.E. 'O' level candidates. I present it to illustrate one approach to the testing of objective 1 and the further objectives of scanning the ability of pupils to 'evaluate', to be concerned with 'attitudes and values', and, as far as 'processes' are concerned, to use the techniques associated with 'particulars within generalizations' and 'the perception of the subtlety of change'.

I have presented this question also to illustrate the use of the grid to promote an essay-style response. Much simpler questions can be made using this technique, of course, but I feel that the question I have presented pin-points some of the difficulties inherent in the bland statement of objectives and the tendency for the questions to be extremely difficult to set and to answer.

This type of question (as in the case of the one I have presented) is inter-disciplinary in scope.

Question 8
The grid displays six events concerned with the Unilateral Declaration of Independence (U.D.I.) of Rhodesia in November, 1965.

The Central African Federation dissolved, 1963	Formation of Zambia and Malawi as independent states, 1964	Ian Smith, the Prime Minister of Southern Rhodesia, makes Unilateral Declaration of Independence, November, 1965
The United Nations impose economic sanctions on Southern Rhodesia	The Governments of Britain and Rhodesia fail to agree on new constitution for Rhodesia	The Rhodesian Government declares Rhodesia a Republic February, 1970

You are required to answer three questions on this topic. You should spend about ten minutes answering each question.

  (a) What is the key issue within the disagreement between Britain (and the U.N.) and Rhodesia?
  (b) Why is U.D.I. seen as being illegal?
  (c) What role has the Republic of South Africa played in this aspect of the recent history of Central Africa?

NOTES ON QUESTION 8
I have used the grid technique on this occasion to focus attention on the situation in which U.D.I. has taken place and the area of disagreement has been resolved more clearly. Except by inference, the statements in the grid are not used within the framework of the question I have posed. Short answers (or even long essays with a choice of one from three) are required; and we would look for succinctness and understanding within the argument-style answers the questions seek to promote. I think that the question overall is difficult. It purports to be concerned with objectives 1, 4 and 5. It also scans 'evaluation' calling on an understanding of values and attitudes.

Question 9

The grid displays nine features of the Peace Settlements of 1919.

Germany's army limited to 100,000; no conscription; no air force; only small naval vessels permitted	The Saar coalfields to be handed over to France for fifteen years	The Rhineland to be occupied by the Allies for fifteen years
Turkey's possessions in the Middle East to be placed in care of League of Nations and assigned under mandate to Britain and France	The creation of new States in the area previously ruled by Austria/Hungary	Germany to pay reparations of £1,000 million (later increased to £6,600 million)
West Prussia and her Polish provinces to be given to a re-created Poland.	Alsace and Lorraine to be returned to France	German colonies to be placed under care of League of Nations and assigned under mandate

Three questions follow. You should spend about ten minutes answering each question.

(a) Choose any *one* of the nine features displayed in the grid and for this feature describe briefly how it figured in the history of the world during the period 1920/40.

(b) As far as the general 'tone' of the Peace Settlements is concerned, how did these settlements differ radically from Woodrow Wilson's so-called 'Fourteen Points'?

(c) How did the great depression in world trade (1929/34) affect the agreements that had been made between the various Powers within the Peace Settlements of 1919?

NOTES ON QUESTION 9

In this use of the grid, information is provided which is meant to be used in some way in each of the questions as well as providing the pupil with a 'focus' for the questions he is being asked to answer. In this sense, the grid takes the place of 'resources'. I think that it involves objectives 1, 3, 4 and 5.

Question 10

The years since the end of the Second World War have been marked by the confrontation between the ideologies of Capitalism and Communism. The grid at the top of page 112 displays some of the events that have taken place as the two sides concerned have confronted each other.

There are three questions on this topic. You should spend about twenty minutes answering them.

(a) Add to the grid THREE more events which illustrate the confrontation

Berlin Blockade 1948–9	The U-2 Affair, 1960	?
The Korean War, 1950–3	The Malayan Emergency, 1948–60	?
Senator McCarthy's 'anti-communist' committee-work in U.S.A.	The Vietnam War, 1960 onwards	?

between Capitalism and Communism; and for each give a brief description of the event you have chosen.

(b) In what ways are the wars in Korea and Vietnam similar?

(c) Describe one situation in which the tension between the two sides was relieved, if only temporarily.

NOTES ON QUESTION 10

This question uses the 'incomplete' grid technique. It has many uses in seeking perception of concepts and knowledge (of a variety of types). I think that it is concerned with Objective 1 in the main. The questions I have posed also involve the processes of comparison and evaluation of situations within the context of 'tension'. Like other uses of the grid, it focuses attention on the topic we are introducing in the examination; and this technique can be used to help the pupil evaluate original material, e.g. documents, press-cuttings, etc.

Question 11

The grid presents some of the key features concerning the build-up to and the course of the Civil War in Spain.

Spain becomes a Republic, 1931	Victory at the elections for the Popular Front Parties, 1936	?	General Franco returns from exile to lead army's attack on Government, 1936
Government forces defend Madrid with success, 1936–7	Non-intervention Agreement signed by Britain, France, Germany, Italy, Portugal and Russia, 1937	March, 1937, 80,000 Italian 30,000 German under Franco's orders	Formation of International Brigades to help Republican forces
German aircraft bomb Guernica heavily	Almeria bombarded by German warship	Spring, 1939, Franco's forces capture Madrid and Barcelona	Spain lost one million dead or exiled

There are *four* questions based on this topic. You should spend about fifteen minutes answering them.

(a) Compose a statement which would be placed in the space in the grid that contains the question mark and which would be in the context of the story the grid points to.

(b) Briefly describe why you think that Britain took such an important part in obtaining the consent of the various nations concerned to the Non-intervention Agreement, 1937.

(c) From the factors mentioned in the grid, choose those which you consider were factors which helped Franco's victory.

(d) Underline the answer which you think meets the question that follows:
    Politically speaking, were the Popular Front Parties
     (i) Left wing, socialistic
     (ii) Right wing, fascist
     (iii) Left wing, fascist
     (iv) Right wing, socialistic?

NOTES ON QUESTION 11
This is a mixed bag of techniques using the grid. The questions show some of the pitfalls of using such a mixture, but I think that variety might achieve a question which can span a variety of objectives with some benefit.

Question 12
The grid presents some of the events of the period 1917/56 in relation to the Middle East. *Two* questions are based on them. You should spend about five minutes answering them.

1 The victory of British forces over Turkey in the Palestine area in 1917	2 The Balfour Declaration, 1917	3 Woodrow Wilson's Fourteen Points for Peace Settlement, 1919	4 The declaration by the League of Nations that Palestine was to be the Jewish National Home, 1922
5 The British Mandate of Palestine, 1919-48	6 Settlement of Jews in Palestine especially as a result of the Nazi persecution of the Jews	7 The victory of Allied Forces over Axis Powers in North Africa, 1942-43	8 The funding of Zionist operations by American sympathizers
9 The abdication of King Farouk and creation of Republic of Egypt 1952	10 The withdrawal of British troops and government from Palestine, 1948	11 The success of the U.N. Truce Commission in	12 The Suez Affair, 1956
13	14	15	16
?	?	?	?

(*a*) Which of the statments contained in the grid were factors involved in the formation of the State of Israel? Refer to the statements by using the numbers they have been given in the grid.

(*b*) Four of the boxes in the grid contain question-marks. Numbering them 13, 14, 15 and 16 respectively, write down four events which are appropriate to this topic and which have occurred during or since 1956.

NOTES ON QUESTION 12

This is another variant of the use of the grid technique. It is now approaching the use of 'multiple-choice' type questions. It contains a great deal for a relatively 'small' response, but it permits a wider range than orthodox multiple-choice questions. The 'complete the grid' request is useful if the material gives sufficient information by way of a lead. It involves Objective 1 mainly; and also seeks 'judgment'.

Question 13

There are *three* parts to this question.
Four of the Federations created since 1950 are:

1 The Central African Federation
2 The Federation of the West Indies
3 The Federation of Malaysia
4 The Federation of Nigeria

(*a*) Which of these four Federations still exists in the form it took when it was created?
Write the name of the Federation you choose in your answer book.

(*b*) Choose any one of these four Federations, and describe briefly some of the events concerning it which took place during the 1960s.

(*c*) What is the meaning of the word 'federation' in this political context?

You should spend about ten minutes answering this question with its three **parts.**

NOTES ON QUESTION 13

This technique uses a form of multiple-choice item and promotes three different types of question. As it stands, this question is concerned with Objectives 1 and 5.

Question 14

There are *two* parts to this question.

(*a*) Which of the following statements concerning the U.S.A., U.S.S.R., the United Kingdom, Communist China, and France is *true* (rule a line underneath the statement you choose):

1 All are members of the United Nations Security Council.
2 All are members of the 'Nuclear Club' having manufactured and tested nuclear bombs.
3 All are members of the Truce Commission based at Panmunjon, Korea.

4 All are members of the World Bank and the International Monetary Fund.

(*b*) Briefly give your reasons for rejecting the other three statements.

NOTES ON QUESTION 14

I think that this is an important type of question. By backing up the standard type of multiple-choice question with the request to the pupil to attempt to justify his rejection of the apparently incorrect statement, we have a vehicle for gaining a greater degree awareness of his understanding of the period, event, situation, processes, etc. It should take no more than five minutes to complete. I think that it can be used to scan the range of abilities and attitudes (see Bloom's *Taxonomies: Cognitive and Affective*); and although primarily concerned with our Objective 1, a vehicle exists in this technique to assess all of the objectives we have produced.

Question 15

In your opinion, are the following statements about immigration and emigration (*a*) 'completely true', (*b*) 'partly true', or (*c*) 'completely untrue'? Write the word *yes* in the appropriate column alongside each of the four parts of the question.

	completely true	partly true	completely untrue
(*a*) Throughout the twentieth century, entry to the U.S.A. has been restricted to the annual quota for immigrants laid down by the U.S. Government; and within this quota, people from Western Europe have been given preferential treatment.			
(*b*) Throughout the twentieth century, the immigration laws of Australia have barred specifically the settlement of Asiatics; and preferential treatment has been given to British people for whom no restrictions on settlement have been made.			
(*c*) Throughout the twentieth century, settlement in the United Kingdom has been subject to no restrictions until 1962 when a quota system for immigrants was adopted by the British Government.			
(*d*) Emigration from the United Kingdom has on many occasions been approximately equal to immigration to the U.K. throughout the period 1945–70.			

NOTES ON QUESTION 15

A different format for this particular question could ask the candidate to write the words 'completely true' etc. in his answer book having first written down the identification of the parts of the question concerned. Generally, this is a variant of the 'True/False' model sometimes used in objective-testing. It can be added to in terms of subtlety or reduced to the True/False model. It can also be used for evincing 'values and attitudes', but then ceases to be a 'correct-answer only' type of question. As it stands, the question is concerned with our Objective 1, although in terms of processes I feel that it covers 'topic' treatment of history and requires not only knowledge but evaluation skills.

Question 16
In the year 1910, which of the following countries were (*a*) members of the Triple Alliance and (*b*) members of the Triple Entente and (*c*) not members of either of these associations. Write down the names of the countries in a list, and write the appropriate letter (*a*), (*b*) or (*c*) alongside each.

        1 Great Britain
        2 Germany
        3 Austria-Hungary
        4 Russia
        5 United States
        6 Belgium
        7 France
        8 Japan
        9 Italy
       10 China

NOTES ON QUESTIONS 16 AND 17
Referred to as 'matching-items', this type of question is basically factual and can be used for a multitude of topics. In a hard test, and I think that the period we are dealing with makes for either hardness or superficiality, it is necessary to place some questions which do not require anything more than an indication of knowledge; although some matching-items can be stretching if the combinations possible among the variables are increased to three or four.

Question 17
In the year 1942, which of the following countries were (*a*) members of the Axis Powers, (*b*) members of the Allied Powers, and (*c*) neutral. Write down the names of the countries in a list, and write the appropriate letter (*a*), (*b*), or (*c*) alongside each.

        1 Russia
        2 Great Britain
        3 Germany
        4 Austria
        5 Roumania
        6 France
        7 Poland
        8 United States
        9 Japan
       10 China

11 Sweden
12 Norway
13 Denmark
14 Switzerland
15 Finland

(Note: A different requirement for the pupil could be arranged if the whole paper were laid out with the question-paper being returned as part of the examination script. As it stands, this type of instruction to the candidate has to be issued on the assumption that he has to return a written script in booklet-form.)

Question 18
Which of the following is associated with the history of the countries listed:

		choose from this list:
(a) Kenya	1 Eoka	
(b) Israel	2 Mau-Mau	
(c) Cyprus	3 I.R.A.	
(d) India	4 Zionists	
	5 U.D.I.	
	6 Salt Tax	
	7 N.L.F.	

Write the number of the item you choose for each country alongside the name of the country in your work-book.

NOTES ON QUESTION 18
Another form of matching-item; and one capable of much use both in seeking an assessment of knowledge and of promoting questions which dig quite deep, for example, an important supplementary question to the one I have presented could be given requiring an essay-style or 'extended paragraphing-type' response on the subject of 'nationalism', 'freedom-fighting and freedom-fighters', 'the road to independence', 'anti-colonialism', 'revolt against Communist rule', and so on.

As it stands, the question is factual and is vaguely concerned with our Objective 1; but it could be used in the way suggested to reach other objectives. It might also be very useful for 'pure' processes-type questions, i.e. the ways the historian works, or the way the enquirer works, or the way certain resources could be used to tackle specific enquiries.

Question 19
There are SIX parts to this question, (a) to (f). Write down the letters which identify each question and alongside each write the word TRUE or FALSE as you think fit.

All of the questions refer to the *Nuclear Test-Ban Agreement, 1963.*

(a) The testing of nuclear weapons in the atmosphere was forbidden.

(b) The testing of nuclear weapons underground was discouraged but not forbidden.

(c) The testing of nuclear weapons in outer space was forbidden.

(d) The signatories to the Agreement included all those nations which had by 1963 developed nuclear weapons.

(e) Britian's Prime Minister, Harold Macmillan, played an important part in encouraging the signatories to make this Agreement.

(f) Since 1963, the Agreement has not been broken by any of the signatories to it.

NOTES ON QUESTION 19

This concerns our Objective 1 in a loose way, but it could be made more interesting through the provision of original material and selected press-cuttings. It is an orthodox TRUE/FALSE item.

Question 20

(Note: Questions 20 and 21 are both multiple-choice questions which use various types of presentation within the framework of this technique.)

Which of the following were features of sea warfare in *both* World Wars?

1 The use of the convoy system with its packs of merchant ships and naval escorts.

2 The development of submarine-detecting devices and of depth-charges for use by naval vessels.

3 The use of sea mines laid secretly either defensively or offensively.

4 The use of airships as escorts to ships approaching harbour.

(a) 1 only
(b) 2 and 3 only
(c) 1, 2, and 4 only
(d) All of these

Question 21

The United Nations has intervened in which of the following situations:

1 The internal wars in the Congo, 1960-3
2 The Suez Affair, 1956
3 The confrontation in Palestine between Arabs and Jews, 1948
4 The Hungarian Uprising, 1956
5 The Czeckoslovakia Affair, 1968
6 The Vietnam War, 1960 onwards

(a) All of these
(b) 1, 2 and 3 only
(c) 1, 3, and 6 only
(d) 2, 4 and 5 only

Notes on the Written Test

An evaluation of each of the many modes of question I have presented will, no doubt, reveal that some are more suitable than others; or put in another way, more effective for 16 year old pupils AND the objectives we have established. However, the virtue of the spectrum notion is that it scans a range of possibilities as far as testing techniques are concerned, and to prune too heavily from the list of availability of techniques is to destroy the operational efficiency of the overall idea of the 'spectrum'. Of course, the problem is one of time and standards. In my opinion, we are working to a false standard. The existing examination is dictating to us the length of time we have for the written part of our examination; and the target of 2½ hours with, say, five essays is extremely restricting. I challenge the validity of the orthodox examination, and feel that I am on safe ground in saying that it is an unreliable test which has won for itself an acceptance in the country which has no foundation in fact. And yet it is this examination which controls our own experimental work. We feel we should not ask the candidates who take a new test to do any more than they are expected to do within the old tests. Politically, of course this is sound operational sense; but it is not helpful educationally or from the point of view of assessment and evaluation.

If restricted to a 2½ hour written test, then we must choose from the range of testing techniques that are available. If we choose we should take care to meet our own objectives. I am not sure that this can be done. If we take questions from those which I have presented in this paper, then the following styles of testing (identified by their question numbers) might cry out for inclusion:

Option 1	Option 2	Option 3
1	1	1
2	2	—
—	3	3
5	5	5
6	6	6
7	—	—
—	8	—
—	—	9
10	10	—
—	—	11
12	12	12
13	13	13
14	14	14
15	—	—
—	16	—
—	—	18
19	19	19

and a few of the orthodox multiple-choice type questions. Without counting any multiple-choice questions and the question posed on 'quotations', I have estimated that the time needed to complete the tests promoted by these three options amounts to 177, 175 and 169 minutes respectively. Perhaps further pruning will lower these figures slightly (or the use of options in some of the basic questions), and if we add in, say, seven multiple-choice questions we might be approaching a fair balance in a THREE hour test. We will have to look very closely at our objectives (and the use of the concept of the spectrum) if we lower the time provided for the written test by thirty minutes.

Aided by an army of people divising questions according to a carefully drawn up examination-grid, the chief examiner will have a chance to select questions which fit his needs in such a way that the end product runs through the spectrum of difficulty. My offerings tend to be 'difficult'; this I accept, but I would ask colleagues to consider the nature of the objectives they choose AND the operational difficulties inherent in test-construction to a specification in which words are used loosely. For example, if we blandly state 'causes of the Great Depression' as an operational objective, do we expect the questions posed on this topic to elicit a memorized list of rather meaningless (to the child) statements; or do we want to plumb the depths of man's understanding of this phenomenon AND question the child's understanding accordingly? If the latter (or any degree of understanding deeper than memory recall is required), then we are in difficulty with question writing, with the tendency being for rather difficult questions to emerge as the instruments probe what is, after all, complex human activities both within the candidate and within the subject-matter we are dealing with.

Another problem concerns the degree of 'coverage' we expect the pupils to have experienced. If we are leaving the teacher to interpret the 'content' of his scheme of work in this period of world history, does the examination need to attempt to question with some equality a fairly wide range of topics and areas and periods within the framework of the twentieth century? I have tried to give coverage to such a variety of topics, but with severe limitations on time-availability which are imposed, this, by the very nature of things, must be not only arbitrary as far as choice is concerned, but also random. This is a serious problem.

Finally in this section I would like to draw attention to the size of the examination script that is likely to emerge from the construction of a test of the type that I have outlined within my three 'options' on page 119. The use of the grid, in particular, is paper-consuming; and should we also provide numerous extracts as 'starters' or for research purposes under examination conditions, then the total question-paper may well reach the size of a 'thin' pamphlet. Furthermore, we must consider the effect of the use of a variety of testing techniques which swing from one style to another? Will this, together with the size of the question-paper, tend to be off-putting to the candidates? Or should we consider the task of 'educating' both the teachers and their pupils to the acceptance of the varied-technique approach with all that this implies?

Suggestions for the Personal Project

I assume that pupils undertaking a study of 'History of World Powers and World Events in the Twentieth Century' will be encouraged to make a series of studies in depth as well as a study in breadth of this period of history. Certainly, the inclusion of a 'personal topic' within the framework of our examination will tend to promote such an approach to the studies involved; but there is a danger inherent in the requirement which we are making that concerns the creation, through examination requirements, of a restriction on the development of relatively free-ranging (if focused) enquiry-based learning. In my opinion, the danger is contained in the proposal that we state in advance any given number of topics from which the pupil must choose one for treatment in the way that we will dictate through our 'advice to schools'. What are we looking for here? We are prepared to give 35 per cent of the total marks (and possibly a higher proportion, if necessary) to this aspect of the work. Are we expecting that the candidate would have spent roughly 35 per cent of a two year long course on a SINGLE study in depth for presentation to the examiners? Or have we other ideas in mind? What is OUR expectancy of this important part of the examination?

Personally, I favour the idea of the pupil's studies taking the form in which he is encouraged to work solo, with one other student, or with larger groupings of people in a continuing pattern of studies in depth, and for the teacher(s) concerned with his studies to provide a communicating linkage so that a broad picture is gradually discerned in which the various studies in depth have a place as 'highlights' as well as providing conditions in which a continual dialogue might be promoted. In this sense, the provision of a wide range of areas for study in depth seems most appropriate; and this can be done, in my opinion, without negating the principle of the Examining Board (and the teachers in the schools) offering guidance to those involved in such studies. Thus, it is the form of our presentation to the schools which is crucial in the sense that whatever we state as being 'examination requirements' is likely to act as the 'maximum' of freedom the pupils will tend to be allowed by their teachers. Because of this, I favour the presentation of the 'personal topic' element of our examination in terms of recommendations which, in the first instance are to be seen as broad, umbrella-like titles which both suggest and promote the studies in depth the pupils might make. To help the schools (and the objectives of enquiry-based education), we could then provide EXAMPLES of the type of depth-study that the broad titles promote. To make the offer even freer (and thereby more effective, in my opinion), we could offer the teachers the right to add to the list of examples (in collaboration with the pupils concerned one would hope) and to signal such choices to the Board for 'approval' as appropriate studies-in-depth for the purposes of this examination. Such an offer would not need to be changed annually: it would be broad enough in the first place to cover a multitude of contingencies for a number of years . . . and in any case, the escape clause of the offer to the teachers to submit ideas to the Board for evaluation and possible approval will keep the offer completely open.

In this section of my working-paper, I have taken from my matrix (see Chapter 5) a series of CATEGORIES of concepts and concerns which I feel are relevant to this test; and for each I have presented some examples of titles which might promote the studies in depth we have in mind. The operational principle would then be for the pupil (in collaboration with his teacher) to choose the study he wishes to submit to the examiners, who in the first instance will be his teacher(s). In this way, we may well begin to see the standard we have in our minds as we talk about the 'personal project'. Under the terms of reference I have drawn up in this proposal, the expectancy would be the 'end-product' of, say, two or three months work by the pupil; and perhaps it would be helpful to us to know the nature of the OTHER studies made by the candidate during the two year long course the examination might well be seen as promoting.

I think that the most important objectives we are trying to assess in this part of the examination are those concerned with the use of resources and their evaluation, as well as Objective 5 and the PROCESSES involved in historical study.

As far as the use of resources (etc.) objectives are concerned, I feel that the pupil should be encouraged to indicate that he has (1) sought and used 'original' resources in his study, the term 'original' in this sense covering all sources and materials which exist outside of the range of text-books and the 'topic-books' which have been produced for a school market as if to supplement and/or replace the text-books; (2) gained an awareness of the availability of the relevant primary (in the true and adjusted senses) and secondary resources; and (3) developed some ability in evaluating the significance, with special reference to his own enquiry-based work, of the materials he has used and, perhaps, in some circumstances, discarded. All sources used in the study should be correctly identified and acknowledged; and a professional standard should be demanded when the pupil presents in his 'personal topic' (whichever form it takes) quotations from the works of others.

An important element of my proposals concerns 'The Plan of Campaign'. The 'Plan of Campaign' notion is simply an attempt (*a*) to have the pupil made conscious of the PROCESSES he is using as he makes his study in depth; and (*b*) as far as the submitted work is concerned, to permit an evaluation of the way he has used these processes during the course of and in the presentation of his personal topic for examination purposes. I would expect the PLAN OF CAMPAIGN to contain three broad sections: (1) a list of statements and questions which the pupil has devised for his self-chosen topic which reveal, both as single items and in their sequential order, the nature of the argument the pupil is mounting and executes (see later) his study; (2) related to the statements, and questions made in (1), notes and references to resources and activities which the pupil sees as being relevant to his enquiries and his exercise in communications; and (3) related to the statements, questions, notes and references made in (1) and (2), an outline of the way the pupil plans to reveal his growing understanding of his 'subject' to a wider audience, how he plans to communicate his findings with special reference to the use of illustrations etc. and the resources he is handling. It will be appropriate for the pupil to make a series of such plans of campaign as his study unfolds in which case I would suggest that he be required to submit with his personal topic all such plans that he has made so that the assessment may take into account the pupil's personal line of development in this particular case.

In assessing this part of the PERSONAL TOPIC, the criterion DOES IT WORK? could well play the most important part. We are trying to find out whether or not the pupil is operationally efficient and, to some extent (and this ties up with efficiency), operationally inventive both in the fields of enquiry and communications. We will try to discern the 'logic' the pupil has displayed in all parts of the Plan of Campaign; and in the case where a series of these plans are offered by a single pupil, we might also detect where he has used judgmental factors in rejecting one proposed line of action in favour of another. In such case, he will also display those lines of development which 'worked first time'; and this might be seen as being significant in the assessment we give to this part of his work.

I would hope that the PERSONAL TOPIC will promote an oral interview with the pupil, certainly by his teacher and perhaps by the moderator. (I see no reason why this process should not be used to supplement the written test if time and facilities exist, in which case it would be helpful if the script produced by the pupil could form the basis of the interview, or at least that part of the interview defined as 'supplementary to the written test'. In this case the PLAN(S) OF CAMPAIGN will form an important 'starter' to the discussion the teacher and moderator could have with the pupil concerned.

Suggested Areas of Study for Submission of Personal Topic

In presenting these suggestions for studies in depth, I have used the concepts of MAGNIFICATION and THRESHOLDS OF UNDERSTANDING. The broad area of investigation provided for each 'set' of concerns triggers off a multi-tude of smaller areas of investigation which can be seen as being on the 'second threshold'; and each of these in turn can trigger off ideas about even smaller areas of study which can be seen as being on the 'third threshold'; and so on. This is one model. However, the treatment afforded to any one area chosen for study might be slight, sketchy, shallow, superficial, or alternatively it might be sharp, intense, deep, significant. Because of this, we should also give consideration to the notion of INTENSITY OF TREATMENT. There are countless variations that will emerge from the intensity of treatment afforded to various studies by any one student, and, obviously, the number of variations will be compounded when a number of students are making studies in depth. This phenomenon will always pose a problem to those who seek to assess the PRODUCT of the students, be it as part of a programme of assessment of course work or one that is concerned with a submission of topic work, project work or study in depth. It becomes less of a problem if the assessment concerned emphasizes the PROCESSES that have been employed by the students as they have made their studies in depth; although it cannot be denied that even within this framework of assessment many problems are created by the existence of a large number of variables within the activity of studying things in depth.

From experience, we can see that first threshold areas of investigation are likely to be so broad in scope (in terms of potential study) that a student of sixteen or eighteen might tend to tackle such studies in ways which would lend themselves to superficiality. To a lesser extent, the same type of criticism can be levelled at second threshold areas of study although it is possible to see that some students might be able to execute such a study which would enable them to demonstrate that they have come to grips with the problems of resourcing their study, of probing its depths to a significant degree, of gaining an insight into the ways their own study relates to other studies in depth promoted by the theme they are working to, and, of course, to the broad canvas of the theme itself. Experience again shows that when a student tackles such a study at the 'second threshold' he is likely to spend a great deal of time on this one area he has chosen, and although this might be seen as being desirable from the point of view of his personal educational growth it is also likely that he will conduct such a long term study at the expense of opportunities of gaining experience in the use of a number of strategies of study which would be available to him if he were to tackle a number of third or even fourth threshold studies within the same major theme. Of course, this is a matter of relativity: teachers and students will vary in their views as to the nature of the studies they will make at any given time. However, it seems pertinent to state that the admission of the 'project' (call it what you will) into the assessment process that leads to external certification has been bedevilled by the emphasis on product at the expense of processes; and it will be no advance in terms of assessment procedures if the History Project creates conditions in which students in their Fourth and Fifth Years of secondary schooling are to be encouraged to follow the pattern established in the early days of C.S.E. when they were to be seen clutching six or seven unfinished 'projects' or 'topic-books', simply because each subject central to their examination programme demanded its own pound of topic-study!

I feel that third or fourth threshold studies might prove to be effective within the World History Project that is our concern. Perhaps I will be excused drawing on the study of football by way of illustration.

'Football' would be a first threshold study; 'The World Cup, 1974' would be a second threshold study; a study of a single match within this World Cup Series might be seen as a third threshold study; and a really intensive study of the scoring of a 'crucial' goal within any one match might become a fourth threshold study. Both the third and fourth threshold studies suggested in this example are revealing of the expectancies we might point towards when we promote the idea of studies in depth within the framework of the assessment programme for the World History Project.

Here are four examples of major areas of study likely to emerge within the study of the 'History of World Powers and World Events in the Twentieth Century', each of which, to illustrate the notion of thresholds, is taken through to examples of studies in depth which might emerge at second and third thresholds. *It is recommended that the students should tackle a number of third threshold studies from an extended list of first threshold studies which teachers will create.*

Example 1

FIRST THRESHOLD STUDY: HUMAN RIGHTS

SECOND THRESHOLD STUDIES

1 Human rights and the Christian church in the twentieth century.

THIRD THRESHOLD STUDIES

1 Pronouncements and action within the Roman Catholic Church during any decade.
2 The role of the missionary movement in either a major area of Africa, or China during the period 1945–74.
3 The protestant church in South Africa 1951–74.

2 The Charter of the United Nations and post-war (1945) developments in the field of human rights.

  1 The development of the concept of a 'Charter' in this context.
  2 The application of the U.N. Charter within the context of the history of any one newly formed African state.
  3 The uses made by any two 'action-groups' of the U.N. Charter: a comparative study.

3 Women's rights as viewed within the context of the U.N. Charter's declarations.

  1 Developments in the newly-formed Pakistan (1948–60).
  2 Within the field of voting in two countries where women now have the vote but were not thus placed in 1939.
  3 Equal pay campaigns in either the United Kingdom or the U.S.A.

Example 2

FIRST THRESHOLD STUDY: MIGRATION

SECOND THRESHOLD STUDIES   THIRD THRESHOLD STUDIES

1 To and from Britain in the twentieth century

  1 With special reference to movements of people between Britain and other commonwealth countries either before 1939 or after 1945.
  2 The development of legislation dealing within the control of immigration into the United Kingdom since 1945.
  3 A demographical study of the population of England and Wales with particular reference to emigration and immigration.

2 The mobility of labour in Europe 1945–74.

  1 The immediate post-war (1945) period.
  2 Within the framework of either the Common Market or E.F.T.A. 1963–72.
  3 Movements of 'labour' brought about by crises in Europe 1945–68.

3 Refugees.

  1 A general study of the refugee problem caused by the Nazis during 1933–9.
  2 The refugees of the Arab/Israeli confrontations.
  3 After the formation of the new state of Bangladesh.

Example 3

FIRST THRESHOLD STUDY: REVOLUTIONARY MOVEMENTS

SECOND THRESHOLD STUDIES   THIRD THRESHOLD STUDIES

1 Concerned with Russia in the 20th century.

  1 1908.
  2 1917.
  3 The uprising in Hungary 1956.

2 Concerned with China in the 20th century.

  1 The 1920s.
  2 1944–8.
  3 The Red Guard.

3 Some common features of selected coups d'etat.

  1 In South America.
  2 In Europe after 1945.
  3 In Africa.

Example 4

FIRST THRESHOLD STUDY: COMMUNICATIONS AND TRANSPORT

SECOND THRESHOLD STUDIES	THIRD THRESHOLD STUDIES
1 Travelling ideas.	1 Related to notions of independence after 1930. 2 Related to science and technology during the period 1940–50. 3 Related to the arts (either any *one* art during the period 1900–74 *or* a combination of arts during a significant decade or generation).
2 Postal services and their links with various forms of transport.	1 When ships alone were responsible for carrying overseas mail related to the commerce of this period. 2 The emergence of air mail and its significance. 3 Any inland (national) postal service during the period 1900–74.
3 Communications and rocket power.	1 The problems of rapid international communications before Telstar. 2 The creation of a system of satellite communication links. 3 The projected future of international communications.

(Note: These examples have been slightly up-dated from the original list submitted to the working party; and the number of examples presented has been drastically reduced in the interests of brevity from the twelve first threshold areas of the study which were originally submitted.)

March, 1970

For further examples of the Spectrum of questions presented in this section of the appendix, see THE BRITISH GOVERNMENT AND INTERNATIONAL AFFAIRS (*L. A. Smith and H. G. Macintosh*) *in the* HANDBOOKS ON OBJECTIVE TESTING *Series* (*Methuen Educational*) *referred to in the Bibliography.*

APPENDIX 4

Some Suggested Themes for I.D.E. Programmes

---

1 *A Series devoted to 'Living in the Contemporary World'*

1 Living in a technological society
2 World powers and world events in the twentieth century
3 Confrontations in the contemporary world
4 Ownership in the contemporary world
5 Similarities and differences in the contemporary world
6 Applied technology in the contemporary world
7 Communications and communicating in the contemporary world
8 The needs of people in the contemporary world
9 Environments in the contemporary world
10 Trends in the contemporary world

2 *A Series devoted to 'Man'*

1 Man the explorer
2 Man the creator
3 Man the believer
4 Man the inventor
5 Man the civil engineer
6 Man the entrepreneur
7 Man the consumer
8 Man the destroyer
9 Man the diarist
10 Man the builder
11 Man the exploiter
12 Man the communicator
13 Women are people too

3 *A Series devoted to 'The Processes We Employ'*

1 How society works
2 Decision making
3 Predictions, forecasting, extrapolation
4 Trends
5 Measurement and evaluation
6 Applied science and technology
7 Law and order

8 Living with uncertainty
9 Services and service
10 Distribution and redistribution
11 Rights and responsibilities
12 Agreements and combinations
13 Competition
14 The Establishment
15 Money—the lubricant
16 Expectations
17 Migration
18 Defence
19 Survival and coping
20 Community
21 Motivation
22 Division of labour
23 Design and production
24 Values and attitudes
25 Systems
26 Research and development
27 Freedom
28 Censorship and propaganda
29 Conventions, customs, traditions
30 Time
31 Similarities and differences
32 Communicating ideas and ideals
33 Growth and decay
34 Obsolescence
35 Symbiosis
36 Ownership
37 Symbols and symbolism
38 Sub-cultures and group processes
39 Conformity and non-conformity
40 Now
41 Markets and marketing
42 Accountability
43 Towards world government
44 Evolution and revolution
45 Myself and others
46 People and populations
47 Patterns and cycles
48 Family and tribe
49 Relativity
50 Living within and with complexities
51 Camouflage
52 Relationships
53 Civilization

4 *A Series devoted to 'Wonderment'*

Bibliography

ANASTASI, A. (ed.) (1966) *Testing Problems in Perspective*. Washington D.C.: American Council of Education.

ASSOCIATION OF EDUCATION COMMITTEES AND NATIONAL UNION OF TEACHERS (1938) *The Extra Year*. A Report of the Joint Committee of Investigation. London: University of London Press.

BLOOM, B. S. (ed.) (1956) *Taxonomy of Educational Objectives; Handbook I, Cognitive Domain*. London and New York: Longmans.

BLOOM, B. S. (ed.) (1964) *Taxonomy of Educational Objectives; Handbook II, Affective Domain*. London and New York: Longmans.

BRUNER, J. S. (1966) *Toward a Theory of Instruction*. Cambridge, Mass.: Harvard University Press. Oxford: Oxford University Press.

CAVE, R. G. (1971) *An Introduction to Curriculum Development*. London: Ward Lock.

CENTRAL ADVISORY COUNCIL FOR EDUCATION (1960) *Secondary School Examinations other than G.C.E.* (The Beloe Report). London: H.M. Stationery Office

CENTRAL ADVISORY COUNCIL FOR EDUCATION (1963) *Half Our Future*. (The Newsom Report) London: H.M. Stationery Office.

CHAPMAN, J. V. (1959) *Your Secondary Modern Schools*. College of Preceptors (To be enlarged with a report on the development of a comprehensive schools system and republished in 1974).

DIENES, Z. P., and JEEVES, M. A. (1965) *Thinking in Structures*. London: Hutchinson.

EGGLESTON, J. F., and KERR, J. F. (eds.) (1969) *Studies in Assessment*. London: English Universities Press.

EVALUATION AND ADVISORY SERVICE (prepared by) (1963) *Tests and Measurement Kit*. Princetown, N.J.: Educational Testing Service.

HOOPER, R. (ed.) (1971) *The Curriculum: Content, Design and Development*. Edinburgh: Oliver and Boyd.

HUDSON, B. (ed.) (1973) *Assessment Techniques*. London: Methuen Educational.

HUDSON, L. (1966) *Contrary Imaginations: a psychological study of the English Schoolboy*. London: Methuen.

HUDSON, L. (1968) *Frames of Mind*. London: Methuen.

JAMES, C. (1968) *Young Lives at Stake*. London: Collins.

KERR, J. F. (ed.) (1968) *Changing the Curriculum*. London: University of London Press.

MACINTOSH, H. G. (1969) *The Construction and Analysis of an Objective Test in Ordinary Level History*. Aldershot: Associated Examining Board.

MACINTOSH, H. G., and MORRISON, R. B. (1969) *Objective Testing*. London: University of London Press.

MACINTOSH, H. G. (ed.) (1974) *Problems and Techniques of Assessment: A Practical Handbook for Teachers*. London: Edward Arnold.

MAGER, R. F. (1962) *Preparing Instructional Objectives.* Belmont, California: Fearon Publishers.

MASON, A. E. (1970) *Collaborative Learning.* London:Ward Lock.

MUSGROVE, F. W. (1966) 'The Social Needs and Satisfactions of Some Young People.' *British Journal of Educational Psychology, XXXVI (1966).*

NICHOLLS, A. and H. (1973) *Developing a Curriculum.* London: Allen and Unwin.

PEARCE, J. (1972) *School Examinations.* London: Collier-Macmillan.

PHILIP, W., and PRIEST, R. (1965) *Social Science and Social Studies in Secondary Schools.* 'Education Today Series.' London: Longmans.

PIDGEON, D., and YATES. A. (1969) *An introduction to Educational Measurement.* London: Routledge and Kegan Paul.

SANDERS, N. M. (1966) *Classroom Questions: What Kinds?* New York: Harper and Row.

SECONDARY SCHOOLS EXAMINATIONS COUNCIL (1964) '*The Certificate of Secondary Education: An Introduction to some Techniques of Examining.*' Examinations Bulletin no. 3. London: H.M. Stationery Office.

SCHOOLS COUNCIL (1966) *Examining at 16+: A Report of the Joint G.C.E./C.S.E. Committee.* London: H.M. Stationery Office.

SCHOOLS COUNCIL (1967) *Curriculum Development: Teachers' Groups and Centres.* Working Paper no. 10. London: H.M. Stationery Office.

SCHOOLS COUNCIL (1973) *Patterns and Variations in Curriculum Development Projects.* Research Studies Series no. 3. London: H.M. Stationery Office.

SCHOOLS COUNCIL (1973) *16–19 Growth and Response 2 Examination Structure.* Working Paper no 46. London: Evans–Methuen Educational.

SCHOOLS COUNCIL. *Project Profiles and Index.* Annually: Schools Council.

TAYLOR, R., GAGNÉ, R., and SCRIVEN, M. (1973) *Perspectives in Curriculum Evaluation.* Chicago: Rand McNally.

U.N.E.S.C.O. (1958) 'Report on curriculum revision and research.' *Educational Studies and Documents no. 28.*

VERNON, P. E. (1956, second edition) *The Measurement of Abilities.* London: University of London Press.

VERNON, P. E. (1960) *Intelligence and Attainment Tests.* London: University of London Press.

VERNON, P. E. (1964) *The Certificate of Secondary Education: An Introduction to Objective-type Examinations.* Secondary Schools Examination Council Bulletin no. 4. London: H.M. Stationery Office.

WALLACH, M. A. and KOGAN, N. (1965) *Modes of Thinking in Young Children.* New York: Holt, Rinehart and Winston.

WARWICK, D. (1971) *Team Teaching.* London: University of London Press.

WOOD, R., and SKURNIK, L. S. *Item Banking.* Slough: National Foundation for Educational Research.

The Reports of Pilot Courses for Experienced Teachers
Published by University of London Goldsmiths' College
JAMES, C. M. and PHILLIPS, D. G. D. (eds.) (1965) No. 1 'The Role of the School in a Changing Society'.

MASON, A. E., and JAMES, C. M. (eds.) (1965) No. 2 'The Raising of the School Leaving Age'.

MASON, A. E. (ed.) (1966) No. 3, 'Education of Children Under Social Handicap'.

RUDGE, K. (ed.) (1966) No. 4 '14–18: The School and the Young School-leaver'.

MASON, A. E. (ed.) (1967) No. 5 'New Roles for the Learner'.

HOFFMAN, D., RICHARDS, M. C. and MASON, A. E. (eds.) (1968) 'Curriculum and Resources'.

Joint Matriculation Board: Series of Occasional Publications
The following are of particular interest:

PETCH, J. A. (February 1963) No. 12 'State Scholars 1962 and General Studies (Advanced)'.

OLIVER, R. A. C. (June 1963) No. 13 'An Experimental Test in English'.

OLIVER, R. A. C. (May 1964) No. 19 'Studies in a University Test in English'.

HEWITT, E. A. and GORDON, D. I. (December 1965) No. 22 'English Language: an Experiment in School Assessing (first interim report)'.

OLIVER, R. A. C. (June 1967) No. 25 'Testing English for University Entrance'.

PETCH, J. A. (July 1967) No. 26 'English Language: an Experiment in School Assessing (second interim report)'.

HEWITT, E. A. (August 1967) No. 27 'The Reliability of G.C.E. "O" Level Examinations in English Language'.

(July 1970) No. 30 'Examining in Advanced Level Science Subjects of the G.C.E.'

(August 1970) No. 31 'An Experimental Scheme of School Assessment in Ordinary Level English Language; third report'.

FORREST, G. M., SMITH, G. A., and BROWN, M. H. (December 1970) No. 32 'General Studies (Advanced) and Academic Aptitude'.

FORREST, G. M. (June 1971) No. 33 'Standards in Subjects at the Ordinary Level of the G.C.E., June 1970'.

FORREST, G. M., and SMITH, G. A. (November 1972) No. 34 'Standards in Subjects at the Ordinary Level of the G.C.E., June 1971'.

The Magazine Ideas, edited by Leslie A. Smith
Published by University of London Goldsmiths' College

SMITH, L. A. (1972) Library Edition of *Ideas*, Series One, Nos. 1–15.
No. 1 'Why *Ideas?*' (Starting I.D.E.) February 1967.
No. 2 'Three Dimensional Studies' April 1967.
No. 3 'Everybody Can Grow' May 1967.
No. 4 'Fourfold Curriculum and RoSLA' October 1967.
No. 5 'New Resources' January 1968.
No. 6 '*Ideas* on Primary Education' March 1968.
No. 7 'Advances in Programmed Learning' April 1968.
No. 8/9 '*Ideas* on Teacher Education' June 1968.
No. 10 'Communicating ideas' October 1968.
No. 11/12 'Starters' February 1969.
No. 13 'I.D.E. and Creative Flow' June 1969.
No. 14 'Clustering' October 1969.

No. 15 'Sex and Unisex' May 1970.
The Second Series of *Ideas* includes:
No. 16/17 'Renaissance 1971' January 1971.
No. 18 'Enquiry' June 1971.
No. 19/20 'Timetabling for Flexibility and the Management of Resources' October 1971.
No. 21 'Relationships' December 1971.
The Third Series of *Ideas* includes:
No. 22 'Broad Acres of Curricula' June 1972.
No. 23 'Educational Development: Ways and Means' October 1972.
No. 24 'Combined Operations' January 1973
No. 25 'Outward Looking Education' June 1973.
No. 26 'Back to the Drawing Board' October 1973.
No. 27 'New Resources Dialogue' January 1974.

The Handbooks on Objective Testing
General editor: H. G. Macintosh (1971–4) Methuen Educational.
BROWN, P., and HUDSON, B. *Chemistry*.
DUFFY, J. D., and WIGGLESWORTH, G. W. *Science*.
EASTWOOD, D. G. F., and HUDSON, B. *Physics*.
FISHER, J. T., and DINNING, C. *Handicraft*.
HARTLEY, A., and HALE, D. E. *Statistics*.
HEMINGWAY, G. S., and MATTEN, A. E. *Economics*.
HOLM, J., and MATTEN, A. E. *Religious Studies*.
LAWRENCE, A. E., and ATHERFOLD, F. J. *Mathematics*.
LONG, A., and ALLISON, R. *Geography*.
NOBBS, J. N., and WALTON, M. *Civics*.
PARK, B., and SIMPSON, J. D. *French*.
QUINN, J. G., and MACINTOSH, H. G. *British History 1783 onwards*.
QUINN, J. G., and MACINTOSH, H. G. *Economic and Social History 1760 onwards*.
QUINN, J. G., and MACINTOSH, H. G. *European History 1789–1945*.
QUINN, J. G., and MACINTOSH, H. G. *World History 1918–70*.
SMITH, J. O., and NEALE, B. E. *Biology*.
SMITH, L. A., and MACINTOSH, H. G. *The British Government and International Affairs*.
THEODOSSIN, E., and WALTON, M. *English Reading Comprehension*.
THOMAS, J., and MATTEN, A. E. *Commerce*.